TWO PLAYS

NEW INDIAN PLAYWRIGHTS

SATISH ALEKAR

TWO PLAYS

The Grand Exit
and A Conversation with Dolly

TRANSLATED BY SHANTA GOKHALE

LONDON NEW YORK CALCUTTA

Seagull Books, 2023

Original plays © Satish Alekar
English translation © Shanta Gokhale
This compilation © Seagull Books, 2023

ISBN 978 1 8030 9 304 8

British Library Cataloguing-in-Publication Data
A catalogue record for this book is available from the British Library

Typeset and designed by Seagull Books, Calcutta, India
Printed and bound by Hyam Enterprises, Calcutta, India

CONTENTS

THE GRAND EXIT

Mahanirvan

Translated by Shanta Gokhale

CHARACTERS

MAN/BHAURAO

WOMAN/RAMAA

6 NEIGHBOURS

A DOLTISH YOUNG MAN

NANA

MAN 1, MAN 2

WATCHMAN

Centre stage, a straw mat. A figure is asleep on it, his head covered with a sheet. A woman, about forty-five, still attractive, is tidying up the room. Or at least pretending to. The figure on the mat is her husband. She is upset because, although the sun is up, he is not.

WOMAN. Did you hear me?

MAN. Hm? (*Turns on his side.*)

WOMAN. What's hm supposed to mean? Get up.

MAN. Nope.

WOMAN. It's high noon. They'll turn off the water soon. Get up.

MAN. Unhunh.

WOMAN. You don't mean to lie around snoring just because it's a holiday.

MAN. Yes.

WOMAN. What nonsense. You're not going to lie in bed unwashed!

MAN. No.

WOMAN. Well, then. Let's get up. (*The man doesn't move.*) Stop fooling around, for god's sake. The neighbours are getting curious, wondering why I've been yelling all morning. (*The man remains motionless.*) You're the giddy limit. Worse than a child. A child cries when it's woken, but at least it gets up. You'll be the end of me. You're waiting for my end anyhow.

MAN. No.

WOMAN. What do you mean no?

MAN. I am watching mine.

WOMAN. Is that a joke? Look. Enough is enough. Get up or I'll pour a bucket of water over you.

MAN. Go ahead.

WOMAN. You think I won't? Why are you lolling in bed anyway?

MAN. Watching my end.

WOMAN. What?

MAN. Watching my end.

WOMAN. Have you lost it completely?

MAN. Dead right, I have. But that's what I happen to be doing.

WOMAN. What?

MAN. Watching my end.

WOMAN. Yours? Oh no. You're waiting for mine. Loving every moment of it. You're bored with me. I'm all dried up. Nothing left. Anyway, it will soon be over.

MAN. No. No. You've got it all wrong. It's my end I am watching.

Silence.

WOMAN. Tell me.

MAN. Hm?

WOMAN. What can you see?

MAN. Where?

WOMAN. In your end?

MAN. My end?

WOMAN. You said you were watching your end.

MAN. I did. So?

WOMAN. So what does that mean? What do you see?

MAN. I see a road. It's wet. There's been a lot of rain. Has to be somewhere in Cherrapunji. I see a lot of moss. Bright-green moss. I am slipping and slithering on it . . .

WOMAN. And I am there to give you a hand . . .

MAN. Balls!

WOMAN. What?

MAN. How can you give me a hand? If you are there, how can it be my end? You are nowhere in the picture, sweetie. It's my end. You are down here, all by yourself. I am up there, all by myself, slipping and slithering on moss.

WOMAN. You're talking nonsense now.

MAN. I am not. I am really watching my end. In fact, I am already a citizen of the other world. My body is cold. My breath is leaving me. You can't see it, but it is. I can't hear human voices. Except yours of course. I shall hear that even when I'm there and you are here, right through the tinkling tongues of angels. How green the poor dears will turn with envy. In short, I'm not joking. I am dead.

WOMAN. What's all this nonsense? Are you not going to get up?

MAN. No.

WOMAN. Why not?

MAN. Because I can't.

WOMAN. Why not?

MAN. Because I see my end.

   Silence.

WOMAN. That's impossible.

MAN. What's impossible about it?

WOMAN. You will not die.

MAN. Why not?

WOMAN. You're not going to set me free so soon.

MAN. Silly woman. That's what I'm trying to tell you. You are free because I am free. I am on my way to a distant place, far from this world. Down an unknown path. All I can see is an airless void.

WOMAN. Now you're blathering. Are you going to get up, or aren't you?

MAN. You're being really silly now. I can't get up. Even if I did, all you would see is my lifeless body. You will never see me sitting up again. You are lucky, my love, to hear my voice at least. The rest of the world will not hear it. They will only see my dead body. That's what I've been telling you, my love. We must now travel on separate paths. This marriage chariot that we have driven so far so successfully has lost one of its wheels to eternal time. You will have to become another Karna to fill in for the second wheel. I know how tough that's going to be. You'll be free only when you meet your Arjun. By then, most likely, you'll be an old hag. At long last, you will be able to hand over this broken chariot to our one and only heir, Nana, and tread the very path I am treading now. You will vanish from this world. And there on the other side I, your Bhaurao, will be waiting for you. Believe me, love. Our marriage has been a miraculous thing. Because it was so, you can still hear my voice. It isn't coming from my body. It's coming from the elements. I have an illusory feeling that my entire self is embodied in it. The minute this dead body is given its final rites, it will be liberated with the speed of a rocket zooming to the moon.

WOMAN (*on the point of tears*). Are you not well? Why are you going on like this? Shall I brew you a potion?

MAN. Oh, the sadness of it! Oh, this magnificent faith! Oh, the unswerving belief! Despite all I have said, the poor dear still can't believe I'm dead. What more can I do? Only when our neighbours, the residents of this chawl say it, and the doctor confirms it, will this stupid woman begin to lament. Here I am, her lord and master, the man with whom she walked seven times round the sacred fire, with whom she cohabited these many years, the owner of the vermillion mark on her forehead, here I am telling her I am no more. And yet, just as she didn't believe what I said when I was alive, she won't believe what I am saying when I am dead. So be it.

WOMAN. What did you say?

MAN. It wasn't meant for your ears. It was a soliloquy.

WOMAN. A soliloquy?

MAN. Yes. But let that go. You don't believe I'm dead, right?

WOMAN. No, I don't. A hundred times no.

The man rises. Arranges his sheet to make it look like a sleeping body and stands apart, stretching.

MAN. Then here is proof.

The woman starts. The body lies covered before her but the voice has come from elsewhere. She can hear him but cannot see him. She is totally confused.

WOMAN (*addressing the mat*). Listen. I think there's someone else in the room.

MAN (*laughs*). Silly goose. There's nobody else. Just me. Your lord and master.

The woman is still confused. Once again the voice has come from outside the body.

WOMAN. Please, please get up. (*She shakes the sheet.*)

MAN. Fooled you. If you still can't believe me, let's ask the public. Here goes. (*He whistles. A bald neighbour hurries in. The woman stands up. This man also thinks the husband is still asleep.*)

NEIGHBOUR. What? Still asleep? Well, well. Been playing late-night games, eh? Why not? With the son away! Carry on. Just give me the newspaper. (*Picks up the paper and wanders off.*)

MAN. Will you believe me now?

WOMAN. How? I can see your body here. So could he. Then why is your voice coming from somewhere else?

MAN. Because I have been released from the mortal coil. That's my dead body there. My voice is now part of the cosmos. Lift that sheet and see for yourself.

WOMAN. Rubbish! I really will do so.

MAN. But be careful, Ramaa dear. It's going to be a shock. If you faint, I'll have to run for an onion. And that will complicate matters. The touch of an onion from a dead man's hand is just as taboo as the touch of the dead man himself. Your touch will put me into mourning for myself since you and I are one, like body and soul.

The woman approaches the mat. She pulls the sheet away gently. Bhaurao appears to be peacefully asleep. She sits looking upon his face for a while. Bhaurao stands apart, enjoying the sight.

WOMAN. Now stop this nonsense. (*Looks around furtively*) Or . . . or I'll tickle you.

BHAURAO. Oh Ramaa, Ramaa, promise me you really will. Such perfect weather for it too. Only tickle me, and leave the rest to me. All that needs doing will be done, systematically. But, alas, Ramaa, we are helpless before Fate. Life has departed from my body. I might still feel tickled, who knows. But I shall not be able to do a thing about it. And you, you will only feel the cold touch of my body. That is how things are now. No use denying it. (*Returns to the mat and pulls the sheet over his head.*)

Ramaa is all set to tickle him when two neighbours peep in through the window.

NEIGHBOUR 1. Ho ho! D'you see that? That's called love. The day's half done but they are still at it.

NEIGHBOUR 2. No brushing, no washing. Directly to bed tea, eh?

Ramaa blushes, gets up and mimes closing the window. Silence. Ramaa touches Bhaurao's body. It is cold. She panics. Shakes him violently. He does not move. The light is on him. Ramaa is thoroughly confused. She doesn't know what to do. She calls out to him. No effect. She moves away and sits at a distance.

BHAURAO. Take a hold of yourself, Ramaa. I know how you must feel. But this is the way things are. Our Nana is away. We have travelled together up to this point. But now I am leaving you. From here on, you must walk alone. Follow your path with Nana's help. It will be awkward if I console you when the mourners arrive. So let me do it now. When the body has turned to ash, I will not be able to return to you in physical form.

Drum beat begins. Ramaa starts to keen in time with it. First it's a muffled lament. Then it becomes a full-blown tuneful keening.

RAMAA. How dark it is. The light's gone out
Fate has dealt me a cruel blow
My evil eye has fallen on me
My very own curse has laid me low

Ramaa sings these lines in different ways, to different beats. A neighbour wanders in. Stands listening to Rama's lament with great interest. His face lights up with joy and he shouts, 'Bhaurao is de—ad'. The call echoes around the chawl. Ramaa's musical lament has reached a crescendo. Lights come up. The stage is empty. The mat and sheet have disappeared. The strains of a harmonium are heard. Bhaurao enters in the garb of a keertankar, the itinerant performer of sermons. What follows falls into the keertan style of story-telling. Bhaurao will move seamlessly from prose, to song, to chant, to recitative narration and back again.

BHAURAO (*sings*). As sweet fruit hangs on a laden tree
So flesh lumps hang on bones, you see

(*Recitative delivery*)

A tree, dear folks, is valued for the fruit it bears. So too is the skeleton valued for the flesh that adorns it and the skin that covers the flesh. In this play of bones and flesh, once you are dead, the bones are all that is left. The bones count for something now. It is their time. They enter as ashes into the ritual urn. Do you hear me, dear folks? The body is gone. All you have is Lord Rama's name, echoing through eternal space. That name has supported you this far. So let us give it voice once more:

> Rama Rama Rama Rama
> Sitarama Sitarama

The tempo of the chanting increases. Neighbours join in the chant from the wings. The beat of the tabla stops. Only the melody on the harmonium continues.

BHAURAO. His Majesty Ramachandra, emperor of all things . . .

NEIGHBOUR. Glory to thee!

BHAURAO. The eternal Aryan Vedic Hindu religion . . .

NEIGHBOUR. Glory to thee!

BHAURAO. And so dear people, this is how my end came. A good man, Bhaurao by name, quit a rich, full life one fine day. Rose from a plate piled high with food to depart forever from all that was good. Became a denizen of the other world. (*Reciting melodiously*) When alive you feel pain, and you speak of it. When life leaves the body, you bear pain wordlessly. For even if you speak of it, you are not heard, not heard, not heard. Scream as loudly as you will, nobody pays you heed. All because your breath has departed from your body. Wherein does the life of a fruit-laden tree reside? It resides in the roots of the tree. How long can the tree survive, when the roots are hewn or die? It too will soon wilt and die. But we are not like trees. When a tree dies, that is the end of that. Nobody gathers to mourn it. It cannot be so with us. It can never be so with us. When a human being dies, his dead body must receive its last rites. Somebody must administer them. People are ever ready to render this service. It has been rightly said, God gives to him who eats butter. We burn only if people burn us. We dead are prohibited from immolating ourselves. A dead man's

suicide is the deed of the devil. Best not to go there. So let me change
the subject and sing instead:

> Live your life frugally
> Wear a torn shirt, if need be
> The holes will surely let in the breeze
> So be it, you must freeze

Whether we freeze or shiver with malaria, we are obliged to run the
home. It is a sacred responsibility that we have committed ourselves
to. Ours was a happy family of king and consort. Times being what
they are, we bore but a single fruit, our only son Nana. What can I
say about our Nana?

> A son so bonny is hard to hide
> His fame has spread far and wide

But today we have been overtaken by a calamity. Midway through
life's journey, our flag has suddenly slipped to half-mast, and . . . Nana
is not with us. He is not with us. Oh oh, he is not with us. Only my
better half was present when it happened. She would not believe it had
happened. She tickled me. Gave me goosebumps. But of what use are
goosebumps when the body is dead? They were difficult enough to
bear in life. How much more so when I am dead! To sum up:

> Once I cherished a golden dream
> Of trying hard, giving my all
> To bringing forth for our Nana
> A sweet little sibling, cute and small

With such tender green hopes still blooming in my breast, did I
breathe my last. What could I have done? Yama himself stood before
me, invitation in hand. How hard we tried to repel the king of death.
We even tried to tickle him away. But he would neither laugh nor
move. Only his vehicle, his buffalo, mooed. Then came the fatal

twinge in the heart. (*Mournful strains on the harmonium*) All hopes were dashed. Nothing could be done. Blood pressure shot up and I went down. Come dawn, it was over and out.

> Here I am, long since gone
> And Nana is in another town

The only person present is my better half. Her I could have done without. Nana would have got things moving fast. My better half? First she will wail. Then lament. Then fall down in a faint. An onion will be held to her nose. One sniff and she will rise. Following custom, her senses will return. But knowing she had fainted, she will faint again. Someone will step up to give her a hand. That is how it will go, I know. But with all that, I must note, our better half took the best care she could, of husband and son, home and food. She ensured in every way, that hope sprang eternal in my breast. But what use now that I am gone? What more can I say about our better half? And anyway, what kind of man, praises a woman who is his wife? And yet I must say, Ramaa is far and away, the best of all the women around. She is fair, fairer than fair. Could a man wish for anything more? When I was away from home, our neighbours came peeping in I know. I hate to think what they will do, now that I am away for good. I can just see it. There sits Ramaa, hair hanging loose down her back.

(*Ramaa takes shape out of the darkness. Wearing a white nine-yard sari, her hair untied, her forehead smeared with a band of vermillion, she stands centrestage, biting into an apple. The chawl men converge upon her slowly.*)

Ramaa my love, take care, beware . . .

(*The neighbours surround her, singing*)

ALL THE NEIGHBOURS. Hail Ramaa hail! Hail Ramaa hail!
> We're your very own gentleman friends
> We love butter on our bread
> Hail Ramaa hail! Hail Ramaa hail!

It happened all too suddenly
Your fortune was snatched away
Your fortune was snatched away
And now she's a widow they say
Hail Ramaa hail! Hail Ramaa hail!

Do take care, you poor dear mite
Close your door, shut it tight
Close your door, shut it tight
Let no stranger in at night
Hail Ramaa hail! Hail Ramaa hail!

Don't let in a single shark
Always ensure you sit in the dark
Always ensure you sit in the dark
That's the true-blue widow's mark
Hail Ramaa hail! Hail Ramaa hail!

You're a true-blue widow for sure
But look after us, keep us fed
We're your very own gentleman friends
We love butter on our bread
Hail Ramaa hail! Hail Ramaa hail!

(*The neighbours fade away. Ramaa too disappears into the dark.*)

BHAURAO. So that is how I see it. Memories of Nana creep in. Our Nana was always clever and a good-looker too. Takes after us, we think. Our better half begs to disagree. Strangely, his looks didn't settle till after he started college. What a sportsman he is. He's away, repre- senting the local club in a Dodge n Tag match in another town. Now, as a finale to this ritual prelude to my sermon, I shall narrate to you the tale of a tantrum Nana once threw.

Child Nana would throw major tantrums. To throw tantrums, to indulge tantrums, to deceive in order to satisfy tantrums is a hoary tradition with us. Child Rama threw a tantrum for the moon. We might say his tantrum has been satisfied today with man voyaging to the moon. But Mother Kausalya had a lively imagination. She held up a mirror to the moon and presented its reflection to the child. Thus was the child's desire satisfied. And thus was the Ramayana written. For who knows what would have happened had Child Rama's tantrum not been indulged! Valmiki would surely have been ostracized. For, as it transpired, he had written the Ramayana before it happened. But things took their course exactly as he had set them down, and Valmiki was saved. (*Recitative*)

> It happened to Ashwatthama too.
> So impoverished was his father,
> that his mother mixed flour with water
> and fed it to him as milk
> Grimacing, Ashwatthama swallowed it all.
> Thereby leading us to discover that
> the root of infant formula lay in the Mahabharata.

Nana turned out to be a scamp. He modelled his tantrum on Ashwatthama's and Rama's, of whom he knew. For Ramaa, his dutiful mother, had coached him in our ancient ways. And so it transpired one day . . .

> In the midst of a severe drought
> Nana began to scream and shout
> I want an apricot he cried
> Leaving us nonplussed

There we are, stumped. There is Nana, mouth wide open, yelling for an apricot. Rama, Ashwatthama and our Nana, that was the triangle we faced. We scoured the chawl, no apricot to be had. Nana would not stop yelling. And so I yelled right back: You're yelling for an apricot as though you've never set eyes on one. He yelled even louder:

I haven't, I haven't. Ramaa backed him. He hasn't, she said. Never has an apricot entered this house. Nana didn't know what an apricot looked like. Dear people, what could we have done? Brought up on the Mahabharata and the Ramayana, we did what had been done before. We cheated the child.

> Rising on the morrow
> To the market I did go
> A jamun berry there I bought
> And said, here's your apricot

That is what I did. Gave Nana a jamun for an apricot. Nana laughed in joy. I still hear his innocent laugh. Innocence vanishes later in life. If we laugh, our laughter gets laughed at. As children, we are permitted to cry, as long and as much as we want even if it's only a needle that's pricked us. As adults we learn to bear the pain. We say our tears are tears of joy. We struggle to cover pain with laughter. We insist nothing is the matter with us. Nothing will ever be the matter with us. This then is Nana's story, Rama's story and consequently, my story. As the prelude to this sermon ends, we must pause, rest and take God's name. We do that when we are alive. But as we journey to the other world, our chanting acquires more energy. For there is nothing else to do.

> Why wait then, let us chant his name
> Panduranga, Panduranga
>
> All knowledge and all the arts
> We know them off by heart
> Yet we gain no knowledge of
> Panduranga, Panduranga
>
> Sadhus, saints have all attained
> Salvation from this world of pain

Eknath, Namdeo, both are saved
Panduranga, Panduranga

(*The chanting gains momentum and intensity till it reaches a crescendo and stops. A neighbour enters to complete the ritual prelude. He garlands Bhaurao, smears black ash on his forehead and on the foreheads of his accompanists and exits.*)

A grave problem has arisen. It comes like God's gift to my neighbours. My final breath has been drawn. Ramaa sits alone at home. Nana is away in a distant town. That's the general arrangement. My last rites depend on Nana's return. How did my neighbours organize my last journey? What transpired along the way? Were there hitches, were there none? Who was happy, who was not? Who was fearful, who was fraught? Whatever it was, in their heart of hearts, each one remained indifferent. This is a tale that must be told. It is towards that end that I have begun my sermon, titled 'The Grand Exit'. What else could I do, when events and people, turned my death into a grand exit? Look, look how our neighbours, our gentleman friends, console our better half, how they coax her and lead her indoors. They've become expert at burning bodies. Their hands are calloused with the ropes they have tightened around dead men's biers. The chawl has not seen a death in years. News of my death has been like a shower of rain to their parched ears. (*In tune*) Joy oh joy, goes their song, Bhaurao is dead, Bhaurao is gone. A minor actor's grand exit. Preparations are now underway, to bear my dead body away in a spectacular cavalcade.

An elderly neighbour enters, accompanied by a young man.

ELDERLY NEIGHBOUR. This event is of a kind that would make anybody nervous. However, we must remain calm and see it through. Bhaurao's wife has given us money. Go and fetch the things we need. Take the list from my room. Buy everything that's on it. The shop is open day and night. Inspect the stuff carefully before you buy it. These days, they'll cheat you with anything at all. Be sure to bring the stuff in a tonga, not by rickshaw. Rickshaws are too small for bamboos. You can't hold them upright or across. When Chowgule's old woman died, his nephew decided to do things in style. He brought the bamboos in a rickshaw, holding them crosswise if you please. By the time he got home, they were reduced to stumps. Tongas work better. It's also a way to support tongawalas. Now the clay pot. Best to go for one that's underbaked. Or one with a hole. They break more easily. Plus, you get a discount.

I must tell you about the clay pot Dattu bought, rascal that he is. His grandmother died. He could never get along with his father. And so he bought a pot that had been sprayed with cement water. His father trudged round and round the pyre carrying a pot that refused to break. Finally, they had to get the watchman to pound it with a pestle.

BHAURAO. Such was the advice, such the anecdotes that were doled out. The guru–disciple relationship is part of our ancient heritage. To gift your knowledge to another is the most meritorious thing you can do. Moreover, what is a guru? He is an ascetic. He expects no earthly benefits from his meritorious deeds. And so it has been said,

> They are men of saintly virtue
> Whose knowledge is sublime and pure
> Whose deeds are acts of simple love
> Detached from the fruit they bear

Young Chintya ran off. He ran off to buy stuff for my cremation. Another was about to run to the crematorium with the permission paper when . . .

Elderly neighbour returns with a doltish-looking young man.

ELDERLY NEIGHBOUR. And listen, keep your wits about you. Tell him to give you wood that is bone dry. If it's damp, get half a maund more.

But on no account, not even on pain of death, will you cut down on the number of cowdung pats you buy. Get it? And tell him not to short-change you on the kerosene. We need at least six beer bottles full. Tell him to treat this as his father's funeral and choose the goods accordingly. Then call the priest. Just mention my name, and old Bodhe will come running. Lastly, whatever happens, wait for us at the crematorium. If you get scared and run back home, remember, you will not be allowed into the chawl. I repeat. Don't you dare reduce the number of cowdung pats just because you think there are too many. We must have a roaring blaze. We need to be free as quickly as possible, so we can have our baths before the water is turned off. Do you get that?

Bhaurao enters choking. Hawks and spits.

BHAURAO. Forgive me, but I can't help it. The moment you're dead, they rush to pour Ganga water into your mouth. You'd think they would be careful. A dead man is like a sleeping infant. The water must be fed to him drop by drop. But who is to tell them? One doesn't stop choking just because one is dead. Worse, that Ganga water was so stale, it stank. You can't do as you please just because you can't hear a dead man choke and sputter. But there it is. Tradition must be followed at all costs. (*In tune.*) Preparations are over. The paraphernalia is here. The neighbours are absorbed in tying bamboos for the bier.

The following song is sung by the neighbours. They carry coloured sticks to make the bier. They decorate it with balloons, flags and buntings. The elders direct operations. The song ends as they finish, and then place the decorated bier in the middle of the stage.

NEIGHBOURS (*waving their sticks*). A sesame seed was split among seven
    A dead body was cremated by seven

NEIGHBOUR 1. I lay one stick

NEIGHBOUR 2. I lay another

ALL TOGETHER. He lays one, that one the other.

ELDERLY NEIGHBOUR. Good work my men

      That makes seven.

      Two bamboos we bring . . .

ALL TOGETHER. . . . . We wonder and ponder

      If they burn halfway

      We'll make lanterns

      The very next day

      Tie the bier, tie the bier

      Tie it tight, do not fear.

      Tie the bier, tie the bier

      Tie it tight, do not fear

ELDERLY NEIGHBOUR. The straw, the straw, bring it on

      Get the cloth and we are done

All together they repeat the last two lines.

THE DOLT. The rope is in knots

ALL TOGETHER. The knots are in your brain

      Your brain is a drain

      Unknot the knots, that's the way

ELDERLY NEIGHBOUR. But tie the body good and tight

      Tie it down with all your might.

They place the bier in the middle of the stage and proceed to tie coloured rope around it.

NEIGHBOUR 1. My turn first

ALL TOGETHER. Over the head

NEIGHBOUR 2. I come next

ALL TOGETHER. Over the chest

NEIGHBOUR 3. Now it's me

ALL TOGETHER. Over the belly
and thighs it goes
Around the legs
and through the toes
It's done it's done
The bier is done
We've tied it tight
With all our might

The bier is decorated with balloons, etc., while the next lines are sung.

A sesame seed was split in seven
With a hey and a ho, hell and heaven
A corpse was burned to ash by seven
With a hey and a ho, hell and heaven

They circle the bier singing and then leave.

BHAURAO (*in tune*). The bier is tied
Not just tied, tied good and tight.

Coughs. Goes into the wings to spit.

One twist of rope has gone through my jaw. My tongue is cut in half. I don't mind a cut tongue you know. It's the tulsi leaf I cannot bear. Makes me want to throw up it does. It is just as well we dead can't be heard, whether we cough, choke or throw up. Had I been a single girl throwing up, and people had heard me, they'd have thought that mine was an unnatural death. Suicide, they would have said. So here we are, tied down to our bier. And where is Nana? Still not here. It's the first time I have died and Nana had to be away. Can there be anything more tragic? This body is ready to set off for the other world. But it cannot go until it is burnt. Till Nana comes back I will not burn. Everybody is waiting for his return. He has no idea what awaits him back here. He is busy playing a match of Dodge n Tag.

The neighbours sit around the bier chatting.

NEIGHBOUR 1. Heard anything?

NEIGHBOUR 2. About Nana, you mean?

NEIGHBOUR 3. Yes.

NEIGHBOUR 2. No. Nothing so far. There's still no agreement about where they're playing the Dodge n Tag match. Even Nana's mother isn't sure.

NEIGHBOUR 3. I have a feeling it's in Ganagapur.

NEIGHBOUR 4. Can't be. That's where it was last year, if you remember. It must be in Solapur this year.

NEIGHBOUR 5. There you go. Just because you belong to Solapur, everything has to happen there. The whole country lies wide open but Solapur it is. Solapur, Solapur and more Solapur.

NEIGHBOUR 4. Stop taunting me. I grew up in Solapur. What do you know of it? You cover yourself at night with sheets woven in Solapur. That's about it.

NEIGHBOUR 5. Not even that. I bought two. Both got eaten through by termites. You reap what you sow.

NEIGHBOUR 1. I thought we have assembled for Bhaurao's funeral.

NEIGHBOUR 4. Yes. But why should I put up with his taunts each time we meet? He should remember why we are here. How do you think Bhaurao will feel? He too died under a Solapur sheet.

NEIGHBOUR 1. Are you going to carry it home as a memento?

NEIGHBOUR 5. Go ahead. Do it. Lick the butter off the corpse's pate.

NEIGHBOUR 6 (*enters*). Costs the earth these days!

NEIGHBOUR 5. What does?

NEIGHBOUR 6. Butter. And you think it's quality butter?

NEIGHBOUR 5. I was talking of butter off the corpse's pate. You're behaving like a babe with a soft spot in the pate.

NEIGHBOUR 6. Look here. Don't you drag my pate into this.

NEIGHBOUR 4. First he drags my Solapur into this. Now it's your pate.

NEIGHBOUR 5. You don't drag in pates. You massage them to fill the soft spots. The fontanelles.

NEIGHBOUR 1. Stop quarrelling, for heaven's sake. Can't you sit still till Nana gets here? We want Bhaurao to blaze away to his heart's content.

They leave. Soon one of them returns with a ladder. Climbs to the top. Takes a telescope out of the cloth bag slung over his shoulder and looks out. Neighbour 1 returns.

NEIGHBOUR 1. Can you see Nana?

MAN ON LADDER. Wouldn't I tell you if I did? (*Resumes looking through the telescope.*)

Neighbour 1 leaves.

BHAURAO. It has been rightly said . . .

> To burn corpses is to amass merit
> Pour on the kerosene
> Let the flames be lit
> Send the fire soaring
> That's true body burning.

Oh lordy, how is the joy of such burning to be described? You must try dying for it. Verily has it been said . . .

> Build a house to know the pain
> Marry to know that it's insane
> Die to feel the jolly joy of flames.
> People! die if you want to burn
> Burn away when you are dead
> Burn quickly and you'll surely learn
> Speed reduces the pain you dread.

I wish they would burn me quickly and reduce my pain. The remaining pain is transformed into joy when the place you burn in is the sacred Omkareshwar. They say all creation echoes there with welcoming calls. But how can you hear them if you don't first burn? Come wind come hail, batter this too solid matter. Ramaa's groom runs amok, mocked by Fate, can't wait, it's too late, he must burn. Or to another body return. Who can blame him for such a wish? But it's not right. To return as a spirit and enter a body that is alive, is like being a sub-tenant, a situation strictly to be avoided. Meanwhile here is the bier, ready and waiting. (*In tune*)

> Everything hangs on Nana's return
> Neighbours play games until I burn.

The bier still stands in the middle of the stage. The neighbour on the ladder still looks out of his telescope. The neighbours are playing a game—last letter starts the song. They divide themselves into two teams and sit on either side of the bier. Each team has a leader who stands like an orchestra conductor.

TEAM LEFT. Digambara oh Digambara,
Shripad Vallabh Digambara.

R for you.

TEAM RIGHT. Radha Krishna Jai Kunjavihari,
Murlidhar Govardhandhari.

R for you too.

TEAM LEFT. Raghupati Raghav Rajaram,
Patit pavan Sitaram.

You get M.

TEAM RIGHT. Mukund Mohan Prabho Janardana,
Subhakt paalana jaya jaya jaya.

That's Y.

TEAM LEFT. Yes he comes, Panduranga.

Raises me up, takes me along.

I look like a stranger, but I've lived here long.

G–G–G.

TEAM RIGHT. Gag me not my choking throat

It will break my aching heart

Time to call upon the Lord

Sing Vitthala Vitthala for a start.

Bhaurao leads, the others follow chanting 'Vitthala, Vitthala' till they reach a crescendo.

The man on the ladder rushes down, his eyes filled with tears, his face alight with joy. He is trying to tell the neighbours something. But nobody is paying him any heed. Finally, he thrusts two fingers in his mouth and lets out a shrill whistle. Everybody falls silent, stares at the man. The tabla starts. The man speaks the next lines rhythmically.

MAN ON THE LADDER. Nana is here, Nana is back

He has come from very far

Played a match of Dodge n Tag

Nana, our pride, our sporting star

The beat suddenly stops. Nana enters running. Young and handsome, dressed in plain but good-looking cotton clothes, he is instantly surrounded by the neighbours, all keen on consoling him. He has no idea why they are crowding around him. He plays Dodge n Tag with them and wins through to the bier. The neighbours are back, ready to assault him. He has no choice but to dodge each one as they come at him. As each one tries to tag him, they console him with the following lines.

NEIGHBOUR 1. What's happened is terrible. Enough to confuse the mind. But a way must be found. This is life, dear boy. This is how the dice have fallen. But the game must go on.

NEIGHBOUR 2. We could not have imagined it. Bhaurao was so fit. But that is destiny. What else can we say? You must stay strong. You must face this difficult test.

NEIGHBOUR 3. What a thing to befall you, Nana. How could this have happened? Why should Yama have chosen to visit this of all homes?

NEIGHBOUR 4. Unable to bear his sorrow, he can only wail 'Nana Nana!' as he plays Dodge n Tag.

BHAURAO. Thus it was that our Nana's proficiency at Dodge n Tag found its real use after I had departed. And now the time was upon us. The meeting between mother and son. A moving experience indeed. As Tukaram has said:

> Let the tears flow free
> They are tears of happiness
> A blessing, a gift, says Tuka
> Your heart's desire, no less

Nana's mother Ramaa is revealed, sitting in the corner and weeping. Nana enters.

MOTHER. Nana . . .

NANA. When did it happen?

MOTHER. At dawn.

NANA. So why is he still here?

MOTHER. Waiting for you.

NANA. Why?

MOTHER. What do you mean why? Who will light the pyre?

BHAURAO. Fire, Agninarayana, is a mighty god. He burns at the merest touch. Once extinguished, it is impossible to ignite him again. He demands that the right man play with him. If a wrong man dares, there's hell to pay. What do you think would have happened if a stranger had lit the pyre instead of Nana?

Women of the chawl revealed, cleaning vegetables.

WOMAN 1. They waited a long time for Nana. At last Bandu Joshi lit the pyre. He had been insisting, let me do it, let me do it.

WOMAN 2. But how could Nana's mother have allowed such a thing?

WOMAN 1. Why would she not? The whole chawl knows. Bandu Joshi is a spitting image of Bhaurao.

BHAURAO. There it is. Let some Tom, Dick or Harry get fresh with fire, and an inferno of suspicion flares up. That is how people are. I am far from denying that I frequented Bandu's place. Only because his father had long since passed. But such a relationship? Never. Although I myself have said,

> As a man of duty, I did desire,
> For Nana a little sibling to sire.

Who should bear the blame for my dying before that desire was fulfilled? Not me, but my Creator. He is the one who sends us down. He is the one who calls us up. We are born to obey his orders.

But no. Not by a long chalk do I share a deeper bond with Bandu Joshi. I give you my most solemn assurance. I swear by God I shall tell the truth. And particularly now that I am no more. I am free. I have neither fear nor greed. Neither ambition nor desire. Only a wish to tell it as it happened. Call it my very last wish. I shall tell the truth. Nothing but the truth. I will admit that Bandu's mother was my friend. Beyond that, there was nothing between us.

But, look, what a twist of fate I would have suffered had Bandu truly lit my pyre for the sake of convenience. People and their imaginations! Panduranga! If this is happening even before I burn, what might transpire down here when I am up there?

But even supposing the thought had entered my mind to make Bandu's mother and Nana's mother joint wives, would it have been all that wrong? A thought remains just that if it is not put into action. Minds are in the habit of playing around with ideas. Why could Ramaa not have agreed to playing mother to Bandu? It would have allowed me to fulfill my duty as a family man. But that is not how the world sees it. To think wrong is fine. But to speak of it is perversion. It is best then, to keep such thoughts to oneself and say,

> I shall make full use of the body I possess
> Filling all three worlds with happiness

However, realizing the full potential of the body in this manner, contravenes the laws of the world. In any case, it is now beyond my capacity to do anything about it. It is all over. My sights are now set on Vishnu's abode.

> For the gates of heaven I now long
> I fill the streets with dance and song
> Again and again I chant his name
> Krishna my oarsman. Yes, the same
> Dear devotee, if you cleanse your heart
> Says Tuka, He will play his part.

Dear folks, behold! Nana has met my better half. Nana inquires why they waited. The mother says: for you dear boy, everybody was waiting for you alone. It is the mother's wish that Nana should light the pyre. But Nana says . . .

NANA. Stupid of you to wait.

MOTHER. Why?

NANA. Why? Because the body rots.

MOTHER. What?

NANA. A dead body must not be kept too long. Unless you put it on ice.

MOTHER. Oh dear! That didn't strike me.

BHAURAO (*loudly while the harmonium plays mournful notes*).

Burn me please, burn me now
Hoist me high upon the pyre
Why prettify a stinking corpse
When all I want is fire. Fire.

Please take me away as fast as you can. Listen to Nana, I will rot. I can hear the flies buzzing around. Why is nobody paying me heed? Nana is here. Take me away. Honour the bier, my body is sore. How I long to turn to ash. Please don't let me rot. Had you put me on ice, my dead body might have shivered but at least these flies wouldn't have buzzed around. Death would have been nice and fresh. Don't push me to the end of my patience, when I've already been pushed to life's end. Allow me to complete the sermon I have started. Send me on my way, make it fast. Make it quick. Once I am ash, you can do your own thing. These poor people have waited too long. Don't make it worse by letting me stink. Raise me to your shoulders, lift me, heave!

The neighbours come together. The harmonium plays a mournful tune. Two neighbours drag Nana out.

NEIGHBOUR 1. Here take this. (*Forces the clay pot into Nana's hand.*) Walk, eyes front. Don't turn, don't look back.

ALL TOGETHER. Come on, fellows, let's lift the bier.

They lift the bier. They walk around the stage with it. The pallbearers stop constantly to change shoulders. Fed up, Nana turns to look back. The man walking beside him screws his head round. The bier disappears.

BHAURAO. At last, I am moving. Salvation will follow. The crematorium is a bit of a walk. When it came into view, I felt the joy of a man who has come at last to the head of a milk queue. I look at the old familiar road for the last time. Nana is walking ahead but turning back again and again. His feet drag. His legs, like mine, have turned to lead. They slow him down. But he will soon get used to their heaviness and begin

to walk as he did before. There it is, the crematorium. I can see the
surrounding hedge. The bier approaches. It is set down close to the
gate. (*The neighbours arrive. They set the bier down. The men who are
in front go to the back. The men at the back come to the front.*) This
ritual is called turning the bier. Who knows why it is done. If it is
done on a slope, it could spell disaster. That said, what has to be done
must be done. The bier must turn. That is the custom. Custom is
God's word. Nothing can be done about it. I have this urge to get up
and lay down with my head pointing the other way. Fooled you! I'll
say. But how is that to be done with me stone dead! So let me go along
with custom, about which it has been rightly said . . .

What the father does, whatever it be,
Goes by the name of custom, you see.
The same is then followed to a tee
By common folk like you and me.

Walk in the footsteps of your father. Become like him. Wear his
boots even if they are larger than your feet. If they pinch, keep them
on till your skin hardens. That way, even when the father is gone, he
is still present. This thought pumps you with more energy as you
walk with the bier. They do their bier turning with such vigour, with
this one going back, that one coming forward, that the dead man
thinks he is on a ferris wheel while the mourners sit still and watch.
No wonder it has been said . . .

This is how things should be
Never give up what's customary
Practise it particularly
To please the saints.

You are obliged to take part in the rites of your chosen religion. Walking
around the bier, for example. Never forget to do it. Men of virtue in

particular, must remember this. Sages have no choice but to practise customs. Customs have such a hold on people's minds that if by chance the mourners had forgotten the front-to-back, back-to-front routine and cremated me, they would have had to make Nana lie down and do it with him in place of me. That would have been the birth of a brand-new custom. For what can be said of those who know best? How long would it take them to declare, 'If the father's gone, go around the son'?

And so, the bier has stopped at the gates of the crematorium. Nana stands by. Why has Nana stopped? There is hardly any traffic going in and out. Why then has Nana stopped? That is now the subject of discussion.

NEIGHBOUR 1. There, there, Nana. Be brave. We are at the tail end now. Come. Good boy. Light the pyre quickly and we'll be free to go home.

NANA. True enough. I too shall be free when I light the pyre.

NEIGHBOUR 1. Attaboy. Move on then. You should not keep a body languishing for too long. Even Bhaurao would not like it.

NANA. That too is true. But I cannot proceed.

NEIGHBOUR 1. Why not for God's sake?

NANA. Read that notice. Besides, the gate has a lock as big as your head on it.

NEIGHBOUR 1. Is that right? Where is our man? (*Goes into the wings and drags out the dolt who was sent ahead with the permission paper.*) Sleep, will you? You come to the crematorium to sleep? Where's all the stuff?

DOLT. Don't get mad at me. There's no timber shop here.

NEIGHBOUR 1. Have you taken one too many? How can it not be there?

DOLT. Well, it isn't. We've been punished for our ignorance. Read the notice.

NEIGHBOUR 1 (*reads the notice*). That's done it. We are sunk.

The others: What's that? What's happened? What does it say? The man silences them with a gesture.

NEIGHBOUR 1. Here's what it says: 'This crematorium has been closed by the municipal corporation as of midnight yesterday. The ownership has passed into private hands. The plot has been returned to those who received it as a reward in Peshwa times. Citizens are therefore forbidden from burning their dead here. It was in view of the love the citizens bear for this place that it was decided to undertake the transaction without previous notice. Half the plot will soon be developed as a road while the other half will go to its private owners.

'However, in order to enable citizens to burn their dead, the municipal corporation has created a sophisticated new crematorium outside the city limits. That crematorium will soon be formally inaugurated. Arrangements have been made in this sophisticated crematorium for burning dead bodies in electric incinerators instead of on firewood. Needless to say, arrangements to do the latter will continue to be available to citizens till they grow sick of the practice. Citizens who burn their dead in the incinerators, will be able to collect ashes within 25 minutes. Plastic bags will be provided free of charge for the same. A beautiful garden has been laid out around the crematorium and living quarters have been built for officiating priests.'

NANA. May I ask . . .

NEIGHBOUR 1. Don't interrupt, please. 'Further, there are plans to start a restaurant on the premises for which sealed tenders will soon be invited.'

What a treat. Imagine. The corpse is burning, and you are sitting comfortably, sipping coffee and waiting for the skull to crack.

Everybody breaks into a babble of excitement, discussing the virtues of the new crematorium while Nana sits in a corner, ignored.

BHAURAO. Events have taken an unexpected turn. It is now certain that my body will rot. I fervently hope it does. That, if nothing else, will release me.

> The crematorium has moved far away
> A body lies in agony, as night turns to day.

I have lost all interest in the burning of my body. Had the municipal corporation at least given advance notice, I could have steeled myself to burn in the new crematorium. But this is where my heart belongs. This is where I wish to burn. Listen to me, dear neighbours. I have given my shoulder to your kith and kin. Don't do me an injustice now.

The mourners are still at their discussion.

NEIGHBOUR 1. So?

NEIGHBOUR 2. So nothing. Fetch an ambulance and let's move from here.

All of them say the same line to Nana and hurry away. 'Nana, wait here. Don't look back. We'll come back with an ambulance.' The stage is empty except for Bhaurao and Nana. Bhaurao coughs. Nana thinks it's his imagination. He plucks up courage and looks back. Bhaurao is gesticulating. Nana approaches him fearfully, then mimes cutting the ropes that tie Bhaurao down. He sits up and stretches.

BHAURAO. Who's there? Give me a drink of that elixir. Where's Vishnu? Send Tilottama to me. Rambha can come tomorrow. Why is Bandu Joshi's mother not here yet?

NANA. What's wrong with you Bhau? Aren't you dead?

BHAURAO. No. We are in heaven but we can still smell our stink. Please make me a cotton plug soaked in Attar of Paradise.

NANA. Bhau, you are dead.

BHAURAO. Summon Indra. Send a memo to Yama. What does he mean by snatching me halfway through life?

NANA. What memo are you talking about, Bhau? You are not alive. You'll scare the life out of people. You have still not been burned. (*Silence*)

BHAURAO. Oh? I didn't see a soul around. I thought I'd been burnt and I was in heaven.

NANA. The ambulance hasn't come yet.

BHAURAO. It won't either. They must be having their ritual baths in the chawl. I know these people well. I've been one of them, after all.

NANA. Let's go then.

BHAURAO. Go where?

NANA. To the new crematorium.

BHAURAO. I'm not coming. I refuse to burn there. If I burn at all, it will be here. Or else I'll rot.

NANA. Come on, Bhau. Burning here is not permitted. You are rotting Bhau.

BHAURAO. Come hell or heaven, we will not burn anywhere but here.

NANA. Stop it now. Come on.

Nana tries to use force. Bhaurao keeps dodging him. Nana catches him at last and tries to carry him. But he has grown heavy. Nana breaks into a desperate cry.

NANA. Burn him. Burn him. Somebody please set fire to my sire. Let his skull break in the topmost octave. Release me from this. Somebody, please come. Help me. And if you can't, at least drop the curtain on Act One.

A mridangam plays. The curtain comes down to its beat.

Curtain goes up. The stage is dark. Strains of a strummed tanpura. An oil lamp burns. The light comes up on Nana's face. He sings the following lines:

NANA. May the darkness of evil disperse
      May righteousness rule the universe
      May each living being receive
      What it desires.

    Bhaurao sings a taan. Light comes up on his face.

BHARUAO (*sings*). Folks, it's time to take your seats
      You've heard the third bell ring
      He of The Grand Exit
      Must continue his story to sing.

    Light on Bhaurao fades. The stage lights up. Nana stands centrestage, alone. His hair and beard have grown. His clothes are crumpled.

NANA (*sings*). Bhau is now my commitment
      He clings to my back like a limpet
      And I am filled with dread

(*Nana's mother Ramaa, sits in a corner sobbing. Her hair hangs loose. An oil lamp burns beside her. Her neck and forehead are bare, all marks of marriage gone. Yet she looks even more attractive than before.*)

Bhau is gone. My commitment to him fits me as snugly as my underpants. And yet I am the tiniest bit afraid. The oil lamp is burning. The oil has been replenished unfailingly every day for ten days. The number of sobs this one here emits has not decreased by a single digit. They come at the rate of one every minute. Her eyes have had no respite. They have streamed for ten days without cease. Dear Mother, please. You have troubled your soul enough. Give a thought to your health. For all we know, you have lost weight. Yet there is no end to your mourning. For ten days our stove has not been lit. The only flame that has flickered in this home is from the lamp. We have survived on restaurant food or what neighbours have provided. Now control your grief and get back to work. It is the tenth day today. The one that follows the ninth. The one that will bring ultimate release to Bhau. On this day we will offer a rice ball to his soul. Now get up and cook the rice.

(*Ramaa breaks into loud sobbing. Nana loses his temper.*)

Shut it will you? Shit. She's the limit. No use being gentle. Belt up. Did you hear me? Shut the fuck up. Go put that rice on and get that ball ready. I must take it to the crematorium. Use good basmati rice. Let him have a blast. His last. And of course, the old crematorium is closed. I must trudge barefoot all the way to the new one.

(*Ramaa bursts into sobs again.*)

What am I to do now. I've tried being gentle. I've tried yelling. Nothing works on my mother. It's been a while since Act Two began. And here I am, still jabbering away all by myself. I wish I could walk off into the wings and not return. But you can't simply disappear when you are alive. You can't fly away with the wind. And my commitment to Bhau . . .

(*Bhaurao's taan is heard from the wings. Now the light is on Nana alone.*)

> Bhau is now my commitment
> He clings to my back like a limpet
> And I am filled with dread

My commitment to Bhau sits in my legs like lead. Why talk about flying away? In short, a huge responsibility has fallen on my shoulders. Fallen? More like crashed. I'm like a monkey caught in a maze. But what's to be done? I must continue with Bhau's sermon. My style will be different. But the sermon is the same. The Grand Exit. So friends, this is the state of things at present. Emotions surge. I mean, my mother's. Sobbing is her only outlet. Yet things must be done musically. That is the tradition in these performances. Since the sermon has begun and a woman sits sorrowing, here is our chance to sing . . .

> Who strums the strings of my heart
> Fate has played a villainous part
> My marriage to a man called Bhau
> Was screwed up midway and how!
> Fate has played a villainous part

(*While he is singing, his mother has controlled herself and is now busy cleaning rice.*)

The intended end has been attained. Mother has got down to work. Our tradition of singing our emotions is as ancient as the hills.

> Mamma mamma open the door

MOTHER. Wait till I finish cleaning the grain.

> Oh this life! What a bane,
> Oh what a big long bore

NANA. So it is for me too, cow

> No rice ball even now
> Mamma Mamma open the door

MOTHER. Wait, let me clean the rice, my boy

NANA. Is the rice ball ready now?

MOTHER. Wait, let me boil the rice, my boy

NANA. Hey Mamma, is it done now?

MOTHER. Wait, let me roll it round, my boy.

NANA. First boil the rice. Then shape the ball. Top it with a dollop of dal that you've taken care not to burn. A drizzle of ghee, and it's done. The rice ball is a perishable thing. If the crow eats it without delay, the dead soul gets it fresh. If the crow dilly-dallies, a new ball must be made of darbha grass. Rice balls are a vital part of the tenth day observances, caste and community of the dead soul no bar. So thus was Bhau's rice ball made.

Mother enters with the rice ball in a plastic bag.

MOTHER. Take care. The new crematorium is far away. If the crow takes its time, eat the lunch I've packed for you. (*Exit*)

Nana starts walking. The heat soon gets to him. He peeps into the wings.

NANA. It's just around the corner. There it is.

Nana walks into one wing. Two men enter from the other wing, quarrelling. They are in their thirties but are dressed like schoolboys.

MAN 1. Have some shame!

MAN 2. Whose shame are you referring to?

MAN 1. Yours of course. You think I'm scared?

MAN 2. That's your father's ball isn't it?

MAN 1. You're dead right it is. And I'm not scared of anybody. What are you doing here, anyway? I can see that nobody's ever died in your house. They're all fighting fit, right? That's why you don't know the rules of the game. You should have brought someone older along.

MAN 2. Are you accusing me of being a child?

MAN 1. Of course I am. Did your pop ever place his balls like this?

MAN 2. How dare you talk about my father's balls! I'll slap you.

MAN 1. Come on, then. Come. Come. I've seen dozens like you.

MAN 2. Really? Time to show me your manhood, then.

MAN 1. First you place your ball next to mine . . . meaning, the ball I've brought. Then you make obscene demands.

MAN 2. I made obscene demands?

MAN 1. Didn't you? You just said so. Show me your manhood, you said.

MAN 2. That's obscene? And what you said isn't? Here I am mourning my loss. Here's my father's rice ball. And you tell me to come? Who do you take me for? I don't have those tendencies I'll have you know.

MAN 1. This is sheer perversity. I only said: come. Like: come on.

MAN 2. And you thought I'd go with you? So the crow could touch your thing, feel full and fly away? Why should we have to make do with darbha grass? What gives you the right?

MAN 1. But why did you fucking come here at all?

MAN 2. Because my pop popped it, goose. Nobody comes here to have a ball! You think I've come here with a rice ball for my breakfast?

MAN 1. But why have you kept yours so close to mine? Has anybody ever kept their rice ball within ten feet of someone else's?

MAN 2. No? Well, I've done it now.

MAN 1. That's why we are quarrelling. I was sweating away here since the morning. Not a single crow showed up. One came and was about to peck when your blasted shadow falls on him and off he flew.

MAN 2. Just too bad. I had to come. And if I came, my shadow was obliged to come with me. That's how things are.

MAN 1 (*mimicking him*). That's how things are.

MAN 2. Don't you dare mimic me.

MAN 1. No? And do what instead? I'm sick of this. Time is hanging on my hands. Spare me a thought, will you? My father was a simple schoolteacher. I've been trying to guess at every unexpressed, unfulfilled wish of his. I've gone to the extent of promising him I'll start a school in his name. I said it just to make the crow come. I could have cheated him later.

MAN 2. Your father was a schoolteacher, was he?

MAN 1. For thirty years.

MAN 2. Then I suggest you put a piece of chalk near the rice ball. Chalk. See if he doesn't come for that.

MAN 1. Chalk? That's your suggestion? I've even tried coloured chalk. The fucking crow still didn't come. Please spare a thought for our father, won't you?

MAN 2. Why are you going on about your father? My father is just as dead. We are sailing in the same boat.

MAN 1. Zip it up, scum! First time out with a fucking rice ball and keeps crowing like a fucking cock! I'll knock you out, I will.

MAN 2. You fucker. I've kept my cool all this time, but your tongue won't stop wagging.

A proper brawl begins. Nana enters and stands in a corner. They are attacking each other with rice balls. When they turn towards his rice ball, he acts.

NANA. Shoo! Go away. Shut your traps.

The fighting stops.

MAN 1. I came here first with my rice ball.

MAN 2. Maybe you did. But you don't own the crematorium.

MAN 1. Why did you put yours next to mine? The crow flew away, didn't it, you asshole? I've been waiting since the morning. I'm famished. Mother said she wouldn't take me in if the crow didn't touch the rice ball. If I lie to her now, I'll have a problem with her rice ball when her time comes. (*Sets up a wail.*)

MAN 2. You think your wailing will break my heart? My family and I have been at it for the last ten days. The crow didn't fly off because I came. It went because a horse can be taken to the water but can't be made to drink.

MAN 1. What are you trying to say?

NANA. He said it. A horse can be taken to the water but can't be made to drink.

MAN 1 (*losing his temper*). I want to know what that means.

NANA. Better ask him. He must be a race-goer.

MAN 2. Don't insult me. I have no such addictions.

MAN 1. So the horse won't drink, eh? That kind of language about my father who is now in the other world?

MAN 2. It has nothing to do with your father. It is about the will of a crow. Suppose your father has no pending desire but the crow just wants to screw you . . .

MAN 1. Oh? Then watch me screw you.

They go at each other again. Nana has disappeared into the wings. He returns wearing dark shades and a black gown.

NANA. Shut up, you idiots. I have come, a visitor from ancient times. Black in colour, delicate in build, beak blunted with constant pecking. Here I am, God's telegram man, bearing tidings of a dead soul's desire . . .

I am a crow. A crow am I.

Stop the racket. Stop the fight. Why brawl in a place where mortal flesh turns to immortal ash? Forgive me, I am late. I heard the call but I was helpless. This new crematorium is too far away, with not a single banyan tree in sight. I fly long distances. My wings grow weary. We crows are in a fix. The municipal corporation has built this lovely crematorium. So why can't they keep us here as pets, like pigeons? Caw caw caw caw! Nobody heeds us. This is Kali Yug and we must continue to exist as crows. There was a time when we were yakshas in Indra's court.

MAN 2. Zip your lip, will you? Not a word more. Now go peck. As it is, you've been cawing away in our bellies.

NANA. What rot? How can I do that? Have you swallowed me?

MAN 1. Oh man, are you literal-minded! When we are scared, we say we have butterflies in our bellies, right? Similarly, when we are hungry, we say crows are cawing in our bellies.

NANA. How come I haven't noticed them?

MAN 1. Maybe they are Vedic crows. Now go peck, there's a good crow.

MAN 2. Son of a bitch, are you gonna peck or d'you want me to . . .

NANA. Listen, you! No big talk, OK? We have a monopoly here. If it's rice balls, it has to be us. Parrots won't do. I'll peck if I want to. Or fly off. My wish. Shall I fly? Make do with grass then.

MAN 2 (*falling at Nana's feet*). Please sir, I erred. I could make feathers from my guts and stick them in your plumage and still not have done enough to repay the debt I owe you for what you are about to do. I'll do anything you want. Just say it. But please peck now.

MAN 1. Peck mine first. Mine.

MAN 2. Do you have no shame?

NANA. Right. Go fetch the balls. On your marks. Get set. Go.

They run off, then come back with their rice balls. Nana breaks into both.

NANA. Shit! Such cheap rice. Couldn't you have used good aromatic rice? But who cares for crows? We are already under a curse. We don't even know when the curse will be commuted.

MAN 1 (*making a move to leave*). Well, bye bye then. And thanks.

NANA. For what?

MAN 1. For pecking at the ball. I'd given up all hope. Our father was a difficult man. Died sitting up in a chair. Couldn't straighten him out. In the end, we had to call in a carpenter to make a bier in his shape.

NANA. No need to thank me. I only did my duty. See you soon. But see about the aromatic rice next time.

MAN 1. Sure. Our mother's number is due soon. But may I ask you something? Do you really know about people's unfulfilled wishes? I suppose you receive messages from up there?

NANA. Messages? Nothing of the sort. Mornings, we peck at balls as fast as they come because we are hungry. Once we are sated, we peck at one in every five. If we touched them all, nobody would care a shit for us.

MAN 1. Lovely. I'll be off. You've told me something very important.

Man 2 is in a foul temper.

NANA. Aren't you going?

MAN 2. You took your time didn't you, you bastard. See if I don't go for grass next time and screw you good and proper. You want aromatic rice, hunh? Did your pop ever get his beak into some?

BHAURAO. Sure he did. His pop, that's me, ate aromatic rice all his life. Where's my rice ball?

Man 2 runs away in fright, shouting 'Ghost! Ghost!'

NANA. Bhau. What are you doing here? Did anybody see you coming? God, how you stink!

BHAURAO. What do you expect? I'm a dead body. A body that's dead. The longer you take to burn me, the more I will rot. I'm so weary of this, son. Ten days hidden on the pitch-dark loft of the house. Even a dead body can take only that much. How far have we come?

NANA. With what, Bhau?

BHAURAO. With burning me, man. When is it going to be?

NANA. You've come here to ask me that? First, you had to die on the day the old crematorium was closed down. Our neighbours pushed off to fetch an ambulance and never came back. I wanted to bring you here in a tonga but you made a scene.

BHAURAO. You call that a scene? I didn't want to burn here. I won't, I won't, I won't.

NANA. So why are you here then? How did you find your way?

BHAURAO. Why am I here? Because today is the tenth day. Our birthday. How did I find my way? I followed you. I was right behind you when you left the house.

NANA. For god's sake, you're dead. You've become as heavy as lead. If you had fainted on the way, I couldn't have lifted you. And oh, the stink of your body! That too after I've spent eight annas on a cotton plug soaked in Attar of Paradise.

BHAURAO. Sure. But if you'd fainted, I'd have ripped my arse trying to lift you. What a fuss you created at the end of Act One. Thank god it ended when it did. Otherwise, I'd have had to haul you home on my back.

NANA. Listen, Bhau. Now that you're here, why not burn here? Shall I light the pyre? You'll be free in under an hour and I'll be free to have my ritual bath.

BHAURAO. No, no and no. I will not burn in this crematorium even if I have to die not doing it. I mean even if I'm dead. Look. Did I ever throw a tantrum when I was alive? I indulged all your tantrums. I even got you dried apricots. But this I will not do. Do you call this new place a crematorium where you cannot lie on your pyre content in the thought that your ancestors' holy ashes lie scattered around you? A crematorium should be a place where you can lie with your eyes closed, feeling the coolness of your grandparents' home. Look, there stands the Shiva temple. Outside the temple sits his angry bull. Vithoba's temple stands right beside it. The strains of prayers reach your ears at the crack of dawn. Look, there. The river burbling past the pyre. Beyond is Maruti and out there Rama. This trickle of dirty water once flowed in full spate during the rains, my boy. We would stand out there on the bridge and dive into its swirling waters. We sliced through the currents and eddies to touch the bank by the crematorium. We braced our feet against the wall of that temple, slapped our thighs and cried, 'Shambho!' These are the sights and sounds that make my crematorium, dear boy. I don't want to burn in the silicon furnace of a crematorium built on the basis of tenders. My swimming days are over now. But allow me, my beloved ones, to lie in my river sand in peace. This new crematorium is not for us. It is for you.

NANA. That's rich! You are still to burn, but you're already hoisting us on our pyre!

BHAURAO. I didn't say that.

NANA. You didn't say that? But you did say you didn't want to burn here. For god's sake, that crematorium is closed. You are not permitted to burn there. That's the law.

BHAURAO. It's been ten days since I died.

NANA. Don't I know that, Bhau. Your stink has filled my nose every one of those ten days. The thirteenth day rites might free me a little. But until then I'm up to my eyes. And here's you wanting to burn in the old crematorium. The place is private property now. Oh, what a mess.

BHAURAO. Think calmly. First, let's be done with the rice ball.

NANA. How? There's not a crow in sight.

BHAURAO. Why do you need a crow when I'm here in person? Don't press me to eat too much. My body has lost its functions. I feel very little appetite. Of course, there's the soul. But how much food does it need? It's immortal anyway.

Nana opens his three-tier lunchbox or 'tiffin carrier'.

NANA. Don't tell me you've walked all this way for this?

BHAURAO. What could I do? You've locked me up on a dark loft. I woke up at night because I was thirsty. I couldn't see a thing in the dark. I was groping around when my hand got caught in the bolt of the door. I have grown weak as it is. Life has departed. And what do I see? The tip of my finger dropping off. Luckily, I don't feel pain. When I got up in the morning, I couldn't find the bit of finger anywhere. Could it have slipped through a crack in the door and dropped into your mother's room? Scary thought. But then I noticed a cluster of ants around it and a long line waiting in queue. I picked up the piece, stuffed it in my pocket and ran after you.

NANA. Good it didn't fall through the crack. People would have suspected us of murdering you. Where is it?

BHAURAO. Here, in my pocket.

NANA. Wait, let me get needle and thread from the wings. (*Fetches them.*) Show. (*Sews the piece of finger back on.*) I've told you dozens of times, don't forget you're dead. And don't pester me. I'll see about burning you once I'm through with the thirteenth day. Right now, I don't know whether I'm coming or going. What can I say to you, Bhau? Except I'm not going to sew on any other parts of your body. Ugh! How you stink!

BHAURAO. I can't help it. Burning is the only way out for a rotting body. Are you sure there's no way to stop this rotting?

NANA. There isn't. If we'd been in Egypt, I'd have mummified you. All right. Now, have you had your rice ball? I don't want you whining about being hungry. Tell yourself you're Sinbad in the well and sleep in the loft without a peep.

BHAURAO. Tell me something.

NANA. What?

BHAURAO. Your mother . . . is she OK? I keep thinking I should go down and console her.

NANA. Please don't. Do you want to haunt her? She is enough trouble with her constant wailing. Come, now. Let's go home. I'm surprised nobody noticed you on the way.

BHAURAO. Oh they did. But thought it was someone who resembled me and carried on. I must say, though, I really miss your mother. Our life together had gelled so well. Some evil spirit had to put a spoke in the wheel, the bastard. Couldn't bear to see us happy. Perfect fit we were.

> Once I cherished a golden dream
> Of trying hard, giving my all
> To bringing forth for our Nana
> A sweet little sibling, cute and small

Just as well we didn't. The sum of our life added up to one. Nana.

NANA. That's not the kind of talk your son should be hearing, Bhau. You're lucky I'm mature.

BHAURAO. That's why I'm asking you to let me speak to Ramaa just once.

NANA. No, no and again no. Now are you coming home or do you want me to burn you here and now in the new crematorium? Remember, you've already pecked at the rice ball.

BHAURAO. Once. Let me meet her just once. I'll drop in while she's asleep. She'll think she's dreaming or watching a film. The stage is set for heaven. The world melts away. There she is, Ramaa my apsara, reclining at her ease.

(*Nana's mother is asleep on stage.*)

Ramaa, my apsara, I'm am here, your beloved yaksha. But what is this? How come we're back home from the crematorium? I was so busy jabbering, I didn't realize we had walked this far. It is still evening but Ramaa my apsara is already fast asleep. She is sobbing even in her sleep. Nana . . .

NANA. OK, I'll take my exit. You're dead but you still want me out. (*He stops on his way.*) But I might as well tell you, Bhau. I remember every detail of what I saw as I grew up. (*Exit*)

Rama wakes up.

RAMAA. Get away, you naughty man.

BHAURAO. It's me, Ramaa.

RAMAA. Gosh, is it really you? When did you come? I don't know how it happened, but I was dead to the world. (*She looks around*) My word. It is the twilight hour and I was fast asleep. That's a terrible omen. Go away evil spirit, may the master of the house . . .

BHAURAO. The master of the house has already celebrated his share of life. He now gives his remaining years to you, Ramaa dear. Wake up.

RAMAA. Who is this villain who now snatches away his life too? Isn't it enough that he has taken Bhau's? Please spare his. Dear Lord Panduranga, you have erased the marriage mark from my forehead once. Why are you ruining me even before I can put on the second?

BHAURAO. Ramaa my apsara, look at me. Look. Here I stand. Bhau. Your yaksha.

RAMAA. But why are you standing so formally? Won't you sit down? Am I being giddy-headed and imagining things? You know something?

BHAURAO. Like what?

RAMAA. You look so very handsome in your suit.

BHAURAO. Suit? Ramaa, is this a suit? Did you ever see me in a suit in all our married life?

RAMAA (*in her own world*). My, my! And dark shades too.

BHAURAO. Ramaa, this is your Bhau, your yaksha. Bhaurao. Who do you think I am? Tell me. Please. (*Shakes her*)

RAMAA. Really. You mustn't do that. Somebody might see us. But what is this stink? Must be a dead rat on the loft. I've been saying to Nana since yesterday . . . (*Looks properly at Bhaurao now and screams*) Nana . . . Nana . . .

Nana rushes in. Bhaurao disappears.

NANA. What is it Mother? What's wrong? Why did you scream?

RAMAA. He . . . he . . .

NANA. He he what?

RAMAA. I saw him.

NANA. Who him? Our Bhau?

RAMAA. No. HIM.

NANA. Who is HIM? It must have been Bhau.

RAMAA. I saw HIM first. Then I smelt something rotten. And I saw your Bhau. Do you think there's a dead rat in the loft?

NANA. You're hallucinating. And listen. You are not to go to the loft. I'll look around tomorrow to see if there's a rat.

RAMAA. I expect it was a hallucination. Such things don't happen in real life. Once your forehead loses its marriage mark, it's gone forever. Falling asleep at twilight is inauspicious. You should never let it happen. And yet I am sure he was here.

NANA. Who is this HE for heaven's sake?

RAMAA. Forget it. When did you come back from the crematorium?

NANA. Long ago.

RAMAA. Did the crow touch the ball?

NANA. No.

RAMAA. Then?

NANA. Bhau did.

RAMAA. Don't be rude.

NANA. Rude? If it wasn't a crow, was it me? Of course, a crow touched it. Took a while to do it that's all. I'm tired. (*Sits down*)

RAMAA. Tired? That won't do son. There's still the thirteenth day.

NANA. So there is. What fun.

RAMAA. Fun? You're being really strange. Now have your dinner and go to sleep. We'll start preparing for the thirteenth as soon as we get up. You will go out to invite people.

NANA. Why?

RAMAA (*snaps*). Why? Because we are supposed to.

NANA. Why are you so annoyed? How would I know? Nobody's ever died in this house before.

RAMAA. I don't want to argue. We are expected to invite all the mourners, especially those who shouldered the bier.

NANA. Why should we? They said they'd fetch an ambulance and vanished. I was left cursing in the old crematorium, with the bier for company.

RAMAA. Even so, they must be invited. They don't all come. But it's a custom to invite them. If we had family, they would have done all the running around.

NANA. Leaving us free to mourn to our heart's content.

RAMAA. My family can't be expected to come. They are too far away. My brother did send a telegram, though. We should be grateful for small mercies. Bhau supported them all his life. But when it came to his turn, we had no help. That's our luck. Anyway, invite everyone. And . . . and . . . him too.

NANA. Who's him? You've been going on about seeing him, inviting him. Who's this him?

RAMAA. I only meant everyone. Everyone who came for the funeral.

NANA. I will Mother. Mother, do we have a spray-gun?

RAMAA. Why do you need a spray-gun for the thirteenth?

NANA. Not for the thirteenth, Mother. For the rat. You said there's a dead rat in the loft. I'll fill it up and go spray the loft. That'll hide the stink.

When I say give, you should give. I already have so much to do. I don't need your questions. Now get out. Go into the wings and get that spray gun.

Ramaa flounces out in a huff. She returns with the spray gun and bangs it down.

RAMAA. Yes, that's right. Order us around. Yours is the kingdom now. Who are we in it?

NANA. I'm off to the loft. (*Exit.*)

RAMAA (*in her own world*). Are you listening? Promise you'll come for the thirteenth. No excuses. And yes. Wear the same suit. You're not to forget that. And the black shades. They are a must. (*Exit*)

Bhaurao appears. He sits in a corner. Nana's voice calls out.

NANA. Where are you, Bhau?

BHAURAO. How could this have happened? How could the remaining wheel of our chariot have turned rotten when it had been whole all this time? Only ten days since my departure and your mother has already begun to see a man in suit and shades. I dropped in on her dream a while ago and realized she wasn't talking to me. Where I stood, she was seeing a man in a suit and shades. Not to have been burnt yet has been hard enough to bear. I could have done without this. My Ramaa has turned out to be like every other apsara, ready to dance off with the next yaksha that comes along. How could she have become a dealt hand for any player to declare a rummy?

NANA. Control your tears, respected father. Swallow them. However much you might cry, you remain an outsider. Dead. You are the past tense. We are the present tense. Time has deprived you of the authority you once had to change things. I am left with no doubt that the man in suit and shades you refer to is the he and the him that Mother has been talking about. I get that now. Thanks, Bhau. Thanks. I need to know just one other thing. Was this suit-and-shades fellow around from before you departed or is this Mother's acquisition of the last ten days?

Ramaa's voice. 'Nana, how dark it is on the loft. What are you doing here?' Mother comes into view. Bhaurao and Nana in shock.

NANA. Mother, I told you not to come up here, didn't I? I had warned you.

RAMAA. But what are you doing here?

NANA. Can't you see I'm killing a rat?

RAMAA (*notices Bhaurao*). Good heavens, Nana. I can see him. Yes, that's him.

NANA. Fear not, Mother. I am here.

RAMAA (*weeping*). What's happening, Nana?

NANA. Nothing's happening to you. As for me, I am gradually turning into Hamlet. Why have you come up here?

RAMAA. I wanted to see the rat. Instead I saw him. I can still see him, Nana.

Bhaurao stands still.

NANA. What Him?

RAMAA. Bhau. I see Bhau.

NANA. Who's Him?

RAMAA. I told you it's Bhau. Our Bhau. Your father.

NANA. Is he wearing shades?

RAMAA. Of course not. It's our Bhau. I saw him in the evening. I see him now. (*To Bhaurao*) Why, why have you come?

NANA. Take a good look, Mother. Exactly whom do you see? Suit and Shades?

RAMAA. No.

NANA. Suit and Shades? Take a close look.

RAMAA. Honestly, no.

NANA. You lie, old hag. Who did you see a while ago?

RAMAA. I saw the one you named. Then I got a whiff of a stink . . .

NANA. The same as now?

RAMAA. Yes.

NANA. When did you first see Him?

RAMAA. That day.

NANA. Lies. Barefaced lies. I ask again. When did you first see Him?

RAMAA. In person? That day. Honest.

NANA. And then you saw him today. Did you first see him ten days ago or had you been seeing him from before?

RAMAA. In person, that day.

NANA. What's his name?

RAMAA. Suit and shades?

NANA. His is the name I ask.

RAMAA. I don't know.

NANA. His name.

RAMAA. I honestly don't know. Why are you tormenting me?

NANA. When did you see him for the very first time?

RAMAA. Ten days ago.

NANA. What does that mean?

RAMAA. That means on the day Bhau left us.

NANA. Did you know him before marriage?

RAMAA. If I had, Bhau wouldn't have been your father. Don't make false charges. For the longest time, every time I fell asleep at twilight, I would see an empty frame. The face in it was hazy. That face became clear ten days ago.

NANA. With Suit and Shades, right?

RAMAA. I'm telling you as it happened. No need to tease me about it.

Bhaurao, silent all this time, now speaks.

BHAURAO. And in all this . . .

RAMAA. Gosh, he spoke. He spoke. (*Nana turns to look.*) I meant, Bhau. Bhau spoke.

NANA. Mother, you are a troubled woman. There is nobody here. Why did you come up? Now go back down. (*As she leaves*) I'll come in a while. (*To Bhaurao*) Who said you could speak among the living?

BHAURAO. With this new problem, I was afraid you were going to forget about lighting my pyre.

NANA. Why do you go on about lighting pyres? The affair has taken another turn altogether. We are drowning in a deep mystery. Clouds pregnant with danger have found their target and are breaking directly over our house. I am filled with terror. I am turning into Hamlet. This uncle in suit and shades is going to haunt me.

BHAURAO. Nobody's going to haunt you. If it becomes too painful, take yourself off to an island.

NANA. Bhau, I'm going to ask you a couple of questions. Think carefully before you answer. What was the state of your health when I went away for the Dodge n Tag match?

BHAURAO. Fit as a fiddle.

NANA. Exactly. Bhau, you said you died in your sleep.

BHAURAO. What's that?

NANA. I notice your hearing is affected. You said you were as fit as a fiddle when you died. That means, unbeknownst to us, Suit and Shades has been present in our lives for years. Mother's liaison has deep roots. So deep that your death might even prove to have been not altogether natural.

BHAURAO. Are you suggesting that your mother and that man together did me . . .

NANA. Exactly! Your death might be the result of some cloak-and-dagger stuff. Lord, what a sitch to be in. Bizarre. To be analysing your father's death in his presence. Bhau, there's no going back now. I must get to the bottom of this affair. I must track down your murderer. Wait a moment. Wait. When Mother was instructing me to invite people for the thirteenth day, she kept saying invite HIM. When I asked her who HIM was, she pretended she meant all who had helped carry the bier.

BHAURAO. Now about cremating me . . .

NANA. What that means, Bhau, is that this individual was present at your funeral. He must have met Mother secretly. That is how she knew he was there. Oh Mother! Let's have it then. Bring it on. Let's celebrate your thirteenth with pomp and show.

BHAURAO. Sure . . . but . . .

NANA. We'll call in the cooks. Lay out a great table.

BHAURAO. Do that . . . but . . .

NANA. One thing is certain. If Suit and Shades did indeed help carry your bier, he will be present and a hidden crime will be revealed.

BHAURAO. I honestly don't care about any of that. Please set me free. This has become unbearable. Allow me to burn. Let me burn to my heart's content in the old crematorium.

NANA. Bear up with it a little longer Bhau. Let me track down this murderer. I'll light both your pyres together. Bastard, killed my father and seduced my mother, did you? Just you wait. Let me lay on a grand thirteenth and pull Mother's HIM up by the collar even as he feasts. (*He laughs.*)

Bhaurao disappears. A song is heard. It grows gradually louder.

Rise and march one two three
Say hail to freedom, hail to thee
Rise and march, one two three
It's the thirteenth-day festivity
We'll have high-class basmati
Rise and march one two three
The proud flag of conjugality
Flies at half-mast, as you see!

(*Mother enters with the marriage flag at half-mast, Nana beside her.*)

Rise and march, one two three.

NANA. Do you hear them, Mother? The pallbearers are on their way to the thirteenth, marching in order. Don't let them want for anything.

RAMAA. Why should they want? I've made enough and more.

BHAU (*peeping from the wings*). Nana, I hope you're serving the best quality basmati? No cutting bloody corners on my thirteenth.

NANA. Don't meddle, Bhau. Go up to the loft quietly now. You'll scare the life out of the guests. (*Bhaurao leaves.*) Mother, the guests will be here soon. Look at all their faces closely. Remember each one. One of them will be Suit and Shades.

RAMAA. How could I forget His face? The day Bhau died He stood third from left in the pallbearers' line.

NANA. Ah! So he was here to carry the bier. I knew it. The first clue is in hand. Now tell me. Had you spoken to him before?

RAMAA. I saw him that day for the first time. He was third from the left. How stylishly he gave his shoulder. Oh my! It's not that I didn't know him by face.

NANA. By face eh? Liar!

RAMAA. It's the truth. I honestly don't know him. In the old days I would see an empty frame. I saw the face in it clearly for the first time ten days ago. That face was third from the left.

NANA. Right, Mother. I shall ask him.

RAMAA. Go on, you. You're not really going to ask him!

The singers' voices grow louder.

NANA. Here they come, neighbours and pallbearers. Welcome, Tatya. Come in, Bhausaheb. Appa, you too. Is that you, Bandu? Come, come, Sadashiv, and Digambar you. Hasn't Vishnu come? The neighbours are on their way. Respected matriarch, please take yourself to the inner chambers and prepare the forthcoming feast. It is not proper, nor does it behove you to show your visage publicly on the ramparts of the fort.

How formal my language has suddenly become with Bhau's legacy thrust upon me so unexpectedly.

Dear Matriarch, I would fain assure you that we shall, in our own person, seek out the personage you desire to see and bring him to you in the women's quarters. Let your mind rest easy on that score. We give you our word of honour it shall be done. You know only too well how firmly we are bound to our word, once it is given. (*The neighbours have gathered*) Welcome. Please come in. We are most grateful to you for having shouldered our father. Today's feast is to compensate you for your labours . . .

NEIGHBOUR 1. What's all the thanksgiving for, you pipsqueak! If we hadn't offered our shoulders, who'd have done it? Your uncle? Go see to the food.

NANA. Preparations are afoot. We have honoured your wishes. The best basmati rice has been organized.

NEIGHBOUR 2. Well done, my boy. How heavy his body had become. My shoulder grew callouses I tell you. Big ones.

NANA. Thanks, and thanks again. And thank you once more. Dear neighbours, I am most grateful. There is only one thing I desire to know.

I am certain you will assist me in my task. When you had finished tying the bier together and lifted it . . . pay close attention now . . . which gentleman stood third from the left?

Silence.

NEIGHBOUR 2. Wait a minute. Third from the left—would that be from the head end or the feet end?

NANA. Well, I . . .

NEIGHBOUR 2. We need clear data. From the head or the feet? Decide that first. Once you've decided that, tell us which left? Left of the viewer or left of the body? You can't go around asking vague questions off the top of your head!

NEIGHBOUR 1. Hold on. We don't want any confusion here. Look. This here is the bier. (*Traces the bier with his cane.*) This is the head of the body. These here are the feet. Wait. I have a question. Why do you want to know?

Silence.

NANA. Just like that.

NEIGHBOUR 1. Oh? Just like that?

NANA. Yes. A bit of fun you know. Just to see if you remember.

NEIGHBOUR 1. Just like that, eh? Testing us, are you, boy? We've lost inches giving our shoulders to dead bodies, and you think you can put us to the test?

NANA. Please don't be upset. A man does not stand in the same position in every funeral.

NEIGHBOUR 1. You're dead right he doesn't. The old crematorium was on a slope, so people didn't want to be at the feet end where maximum pressure fell on you going down.

NEIGHBOUR 4. My question is, can we not discuss the third man from the left while we have lunch? What do you say, Nanasaheb?

NANA. The basmati rice is not yet done. If we try and track him down now, it will give us something to do.

NEIGHBOUR 4. Why's that? We could play Last Letter Starts the Song.

NANA. No.

NEIGHBOUR 4. Why not?

NANA. You played that in Act One.

NEIGHBOUR 4. How could you know that? Your entry came later.

NANA. Oh, come on. I was watching from the wings. Who do you think was prompting you?

NEIGHBOUR 4. We've gone way off track. Way off. Back to third man from the left. So. Let's assume it is left of body and we count the man at the head end as the first, then the third would be . . . (*He points to a young man*) . . . him.

YOUNG MAN (*flaring up*). That's utter nonsense. The minute the bier was lifted, what was thrust into my hand was a clay pot, that's what. I kept saying: let me have a chance at the bier. I need experience. But of course, being young I got the clay pot. Nobody'd bothered to put a hole in it either. Why would they? They wanted to snatch it back as soon as the pyre was lit. And I'm supposed to be the third from the left.

NEIGHBOUR 1. Look here. Stop shouting. I tend to forget things. To make matters worse, the old crematorium closed the very day Bhau died.

NANA. And it's the thirteenth day today and still no ambulance.

NEIGHBOUR 1. It took ages to find one, you know. By the time we did, you and the body had disappeared. So who broke the pot?

NANA. You people abandoned me. I was left to do everything myself.

It suddenly grows dark. Bhaurao sits alone, looking sad. Only his face is lit.

BHAURAO. Yes. Oh yes. He had to do everything. I couldn't even throw myself into the river. I was already dead and bloated. Lord Panduranga, do you too feel no pity for me? Couldn't you send me a single-seater airplane? Or at least make me invisible.

Light comes up.

NANA. So that's how it was.

NEIGHBOUR 5. You mean, you managed to light the pyre all by yourself at such a young age?

YOUNG MAN. And here's us. Always with the pot.

NEIGHBOUR 1. Come to the point. Why do you want to know about the third man from the left?

NANA. Just want to find out.

NEIGHBOUR 1. What?

NANA. Who it was. Who was the third from the left?

NEIGHBOUR 1. But why? What has he done to you?

NANA. He pinched a bamboo from Bhau's bier and made it lopsided. He split the bamboo into batons and made an outsize lantern from them. When evening falls, we see it swinging with the breeze in the room where Bhau died. It scares my mother. Her mind begins to wander. She froths at the mouth. Her fingers and toes curl and grow stiff. And she keeps howling 'Third from the Left. Suit and Shades.'

Silence.

NEIGHBOUR 1. Nana, I don't think such a low-down creature resides in this chawl. It's possible that one of the kids made away with the bamboo. But I don't think he would dare make a lantern from it.

NANA. You're wrong. Third from the Left has to be one of you. Come on, speak up. Who is it? Why are you mum? Out with it. Who was it? I demand to know on oath of my father. Of his rice ball. Of his bier. My good men. I only ask about the third man from the left. Who was it?

RAMAA. Please come. Lunch is served

They all troop in, singing the marching song. Silence.

NANA. Who's there?

BHAURAO. I. Did you find him? Third from . . .

NANA. . . . the Left. He'll be the death of me. I'm like a lamb to the slaughter. No trace of him. Soon Mother will come. What will I tell her? Whose face shall I put in her empty frame, and how will I catch my father's killer?

BHAURAO. Forget him. To hell with him. Feed me to the fire. That's my only desire.

NANA. Wait a bit. Let me think. It's all for your good.

BHAURAO. What the fuck good can you do me now? I'm not one of you.

NANA. Bhau, every single neighbour turned up for your thirteenth, except Third from the Left. Mystery unsolved. I laid on a spectacular thirteenth. Bribed the pallbearers with basmati. Nothing worked.

BHAURAO. Will you do something for me?

NANA. What now?

BHAURAO. Go to your mother's room. Get some fresh clothes from my trunk. These are horribly grubby. My stink has soaked right into them.

NANA (*jumps up and starts dancing like one possessed. Sings to a jaunty beat*). Clothes, clothes.

BHAURAO. What's got into you? What's wrong?

NANA. Clothes clothes.

>   My clothes, your clothes,
>   His clothes, their clothes.

BHAURAO. What clothes?

NANA. Cotton clothes, silk clothes,

>   Long clothes, short clothes.
>   Clothes . . .

BHAURAO. Yes, yes. But get them quick.

NANA. I see him. I see him. Third from the Left, right, left, right, third. Bring them on, line them up. One, two, three in a row.

> Row row row your boat
> I've become a scapegoat
> Gotcha there. Suit and Shades
> Gotcha third. You piece of turd
> Pop has popped. Mom's got the hots
> Clothes, frame, pyre, furnace
> I won't burn, you won't burn.
> Frame, bier, shoulders, third
> From the left, he's a turd.
> One two, row your boat.
> I'm the goat, the scapest goat.
> Gotcha gotcha, clothes clothes.

His dancing grows wild. Bhaurao goes up to him. Gives him a hard slap. Silence. Nana calms down.

NANA. Bhau, that's it. I've found him. Suit and Shades. We're near the end.

BHAURAO. My end came thirteen days ago, remember?

NANA. The end, Bhau. Curtains. Finis. Got him. Got Third from the Left. Go, Bhau. Go into the wings. (*Bhaurao makes a move to go.*) Not that one. The other. You'll find a cloth bag there. It says Vanadevi Brand Asafoetida. Go get it.

Bhaurao fetches the bag.

NANA (*digs into the bag*). There he is. Third from the Left. (*Holds up a pair of dark shades and puts them on Bhaurao's eyes.*) There you are, Bhau. You are Third from the Left.

BHAURAO. And how did I give my shoulder to me?

NANA. Listen to me, Bhau . . .

BHAURAO. How can I be Third from the Left? I'm a corpse, right?

NANA. Just listen to me. And don't interrupt till I'm done. Truth is, we haven't found Third from the Left because he didn't turn up for the thirteenth. With the tiny scrap of information we have, even the CID wouldn't know where to look. Mother remembers only his suit and shades. Not even his face. Or so she claims. We want to find out the truth. We don't want Mother's frame to remain empty. We must ferret out the truth, by hook or by crook. You must help me. You must play Third from the Left.

Once it is established that you are Third from the Left, Mother will open her heart to you. The last time around, you stole into her dream. Now go to her upright, as your right. You'll get to know each other better. Mother will begin to trust you. Finally, the truth about your death will be out from the horse's mouth. Er . . . the mare's mouth. Who is he? How did he escape your eye, how did he meet her, and why? Did he come before you died or after? And . . . and . . .

BHAURAO. Go on. Don't stop. It's getting interesting.

NANA. And we will even discover if the Suit and Shades that Mother saw in her empty frame was you all along.

Silence.

BHAURAO. I'm on.

NANA. That's it. You're on. Now get into those clothes and present yourself to Mother. I'll introduce you to her.

BHAURAO. I get that. But . . .

NANA. But what?

BHAURAO. The stink. What do I do about that?

NANA. Go to the loft and spray yourself with insecticide. It will cover the stink a bit. Run along now. Off to the loft.

BHAURAO. Where's that?

NANA. I mean, wings. I'll alert Mother to your arrival and then call you. (*Bhaurao goes away with the bag.*) Mother. Ho there, Mother.

RAMAA. What is it? (*Sad expression.*)

NANA. The thirteenth was a hit. Your stress is over. Why then does your face . . .

RAMAA. Don't worry. I'm all right.

NANA. I hadn't finished. Your line comes after mine. Why then does your face look so sad? I don't understand.

RAMAA. Don't worry. I'm all right. It's just fatigue.

NANA. Unhunh. I know what it is. You are down because you did not see Mr Third from the Left. But I'm a man of my word. I said I would find him. And I have. (*Holds up his palm*) Give me five.

RAMAA. Oh my! Really? You're teasing me, aren't you?

NANA. Swear by you. He could not come personally for the thirteenth on account of a previous engagement.

RAMAA. You mean you actually . . .

NANA. . . . met him. At his place.

RAMAA. His home?

NANA. Well, he doesn't live here. He comes down a couple of days a week. Goes back when his work is done.

RAMAA. What work?

NANA. He has a very large business. He stays in a hotel. Executive Suite.

RAMAA. Executive Suite?

NANA. Did I say that in Kannada the first time? Yes. Executive Suite.

RAMAA. How wonderful that you actually met him. Who gave you his address?

NANA. Who? I grilled the neighbours during the thirteenth. They wouldn't speak up at first. But then they did and divulged the address. I said to them: some stranger turns up for Bhau's funeral and you don't even notice him? Or know who he is? How can that be?

RAMAA. When can I meet him?

NANA. I've made arrangements for that too.

RAMAA. Listen to me, Nana. Bhau is gone now. You have had to grow up overnight. You have a huge responsibility. I'll tell you frankly how I feel. With Bhau gone, I won't be able to live alone.

NANA. What do you mean?

RAMAA. I mean, about Third from the Left . . . I . . . I (*Blushes*)

NANA. Silly filly. Speak up. What's all this I . . . I . . . eh? Aha! See how a certain person has suddenly perked up.

RAMAA. Stop teasing me. Go away.

NANA. Dear Mother, the first time you pronounced the words Suit and Shades, I knew which way the wind was blowing. It's nothing to blush about. Now tell me the truth. Did you get to know him before or after Bhau died?

Silence.

RAMAA. I don't know. I kept seeing an empty frame. The face in it was never clear. It was only on the thirteenth that I realized whom that face belonged to. I first saw him as a pallbearer . . . and decided . . . forgive me for being candid . . . that this was my partner for the remainder of my life. My prince will carry me far, far away . . . away from this chawl. I shall have no worries. No house work. No chores. I will disappear. Or, all this will disappear. There will be just me and my Third from the Left, running together down a long, long road. I'm not sure I can do it, though. Our roads have become too bumpy.

NANA. Shall I ask him then?

RAMAA. Do you think you could?

NANA. Why not? After Bhau, I am seen as a responsible man. Anyway, it's no crime to check out a marriage match for one's mother. In fact, it might even be my duty. I hope to God he approves of you. I'll ask him straight out, when can I bring my mother, or rather the girl, for the seeing ceremony.

RAMAA. I'll go and see about dinner now. (*Exit*)

NANA. My mother is in this wing. She just told me why she was going. My father is in this other wing. He is dead. But he also happens to be the prospective groom. That puts him in the opposition party. Mother and Father cannot inhabit the same wing. One alive, the other dead. I must find out who HE is whom my mother desires. At this point, my father, my dead father, is He. And absurder still, my mother wants to marry my father. I wish I could get out of this maze. But then, how will I know who He is? How will I get to the bottom of my mother's intriguing affair? My brain is totally addled. I wish I could become Tarzan, parts 1 to 15. No need to think, no need to feel, no kith, no kin, no communication. You don't even know you exist. All you do is hold on to your gorilla friend's hand. When danger comes, holler out the Tarzan call. Danger vanishes. And you're back with your gorilla. (*Does the Tarzan call.*)

BHAURAO. Coming. What's up? Danger?

NANA. You have a very big business . . .

BHAURAO. How's that?

NANA. . . . is what I have told her, alias my mother, aka your wife Ramaa. You come to this city every weekend and stay in a hotel. Executive Suite.

BHAURAO. Executive Suite?

NANA. I've already noted earlier how I feel about this line. Yes, Executive Suite. Get it? You are Third from the Left. My mother likes you. She wishes to marry you. When can I bring her, the prospective bride, to be seen? Or would you prefer to come to our place and see her?

BHAURAO. But aren't we already married?

NANA. Maybe. But there's no law against a woman marrying the same man twice. Repeat your seven rounds of the sacred fire and you're done.

BHAURAO. But I am not one of you. I'm a rotting, stinking corpse.

NANA. I don't know how to deal with this. Look, I am interested in your death. Meanwhile, you are interested in knowing who Third from the Left is. How could you have turned into Hamlet's father? But don't give up halfway, Bhau. Shouldn't you be giving me courage, instead of me, you? Why don't you just take a look at the girl? She's a widow with one encumbrance. Goodlooking. This is also your second marriage. Please don't turn down the proposal. The girl will lose heart. The encumbrance has no objection. He will live apart. Once you have seen each other, I will know the truth. The girl is alive. You are . . .

Bhaurao's stink makes him sick. He passes out. Bhaurao fetches him a glass of water from the wings.

BHAURAO. How do you feel now?

NANA. Just fine. I felt faint with too much thinking. I was sure I was going to die. That would have been the end. Father and son on a joint pyre. Like taking the school-certificate exam together. I'll go tell Mother you are coming to see her. Go to the loft and come down dressed in your suit and shades.

(*Bhaurao exits.*)

(*Nana calls after him*). Don't forget to spray yourself. Mother! Where are you?

RAMAA (*coming back in*). What is it?

NANA. He's coming.

RAMAA. Who he?

NANA. Third from the Left.

RAMAA. When?

NANA. He's on his way.

RAMAA. Why didn't you tell me earlier? I need time to get ready. I'm such a mess.

NANA. No more questions. He's already here.

RAMAA. What are you saying? Where is he?

NANA. Sitting in the loft.

RAMAA. In the loft?

NANA. Yes.

RAMAA. For heaven's sake. Why did you put him there?

NANA. What could I do? You were inside. He came and said: hide me.

RAMAA. Whatever for?

NANA. I don't know. I did say to him: why do you want to be hidden? For what reason? You're a grown man. Past the age for hiding. It's a bit off. Come to view a girl and ask to be hidden. That makes no sense. I argued. Oh yes, I did. He said: hide me or I'll tickle you. So I hid him. After all, we are the bride's side. Ours is not to question why.

RAMAA. So what do I do now?

NANA. Sit down quickly. And don't say a word. Drape your sari modestly. Close your eyes. I'll call him. What's his name you said?

RAMAA. Go away. I'm not taking his name.

NANA. Go away? What nonsense. You've been married once before. This isn't new. Bride-to-be is too shy to take his name and bridegroom-to-be hides. It's a proper merry-go-round. Second marriages spell trouble alright. Come on. Out with the name. Look at her blushing. I said: name.

RAMAA. I don't know.

NANA. You're a lot of help, aren't you? OK. Ready?

RAMAA. Ready.

NANA. One, two three, Third from the Left ho.

> (*Bhaurao answers the call.*)

> Don't just answer me. Come down. Take a look at the girl. Make it quick.

BHAU (*from the wings*). Tell her to prove she can thread a needle.

> *Nana fetches needle and thread from the wings and hands them over to Ramaa.*

RAMAA. Please, my eyesight's bad. Why don't you do it?

NANA. Give. (*He does it.*) She's done it. The girl's eyesight is excellent. Come down, now. Come on. Bloody hell, why have you been brought here? Third from the Left, are you coming or . . .

BHAURAO. How can I come? I'm supposed to be hiding.

NANA. You are hiding? I hid you, dammit.

RAMAA. He has a jokey nature, doesn't he?

NANA. Sure. Now will you come down or shall I come up.

BHAURAO (*from the wings*). Why don't you? That would mean I've been caught.

NANA. What are you doing up there anyway?

BHAURAO (*off-stage*). Singing.

RAMAA. Please don't ask me to sing now. I don't have a voice for it. Don't fool around, please.

NANA. He said He . . . He is singing. Listen you, come down this minute. Sing down here if you like.

BHAURAO (*enters. Drunk as a lord. Mic in hand. Nana goes into the wings. Bhaurao sings and dances to a version of an old Hindi-film hit*).

> Hey muttakodi kavvadi hadaa
>
> Muttakodi kavvadi hadaa

In love I did my best
Lay a log on my chest

RAMAA. Ayyoda ayyo amma.

BHAURAO. Muttakodi kavvadi hadaa.

Get sandalwood, the best
Did all I desired in love
Lay a log on my chest

RAMAA. Ayyoda ayyo amma . . .

When Bhaurao gets too close to Ramaa, Nana sprays him from the wings with insecticide.

BHAURAO. Muttakodi kavvadi hadaa

Put dough on both eyelids
All that love demanded I did

Nana, you are great. I found your stash of whiskey on the loft. Couldn't bear the stink. So I finished it off. You've been drinking on the sly, eh?

NANA (*whispering*). I bought it to drink after lighting your pyre. I can see you've got your kick out of it.

RAMAA. What's that language you are speaking? I don't understand it.

BHAURAO. Good morning, Ganga.

RAMAA. You joker! My name is Ramaa.

BHAURAO. But you're Ganga to me. I saw you first when you put Ganga water in your husband's mouth. And I said to myself, this is my Ganga.

RAMAA. Are you going to call me Ganga?

BHAURAO. Yes. My Ganges. Let's have a look at you.

(*Ramaa raises her head.*)

I've seen you, Ganga dear. I've seen you. I like you. I'll be off now. (*Starts to leave*)

RAMAA. Take care, won't you?

NANA (*in his ear*). Lie down in the loft. Must be strong stuff. It's gone to your head even in death.

Bhaurao exits.

RAMAA. Oh dear, he's gone. Even before we could ask his name. Oh what bliss. Bliss, bliss, bliss. I shall die of happiness. I don't know what to do. How do I express my joy?

NANA. Go ahead and sing. Sing away. No need to justify.

RAMAA. Oh my! I've found my voice. I've found my key. Diwali has just walked into my home.

(*She carries a puja salver. Nana holds a lit sparkler. The back curtain rises, revealing an arrangement of lights which sway to the beat of the song she sings.*)

> In my silver salver the oil lamp gently flickers
> Every flame declaring our love for each other
> A golden day has risen full of loving whispers
> I worship my beloved with myriads of tender flowers
> In my silver salver the oil lamp gently flickers

The song fades away. Light now only on Nana's face.

NANA. The end of my father's thirteenth has brought Diwali to my home and I, frightened by the lights, trudge down the path to the old crematorium. I must end the chaos my father and mother have created by lighting his pyre. I lost my way trying to solve a mystery. Set up a girl-viewing ceremony where my father told the girl to her face that he approved of her and left me standing.

I must now tell my mother that he is not the He of her frame. This one is a spirit greedy for fire. A living woman cannot marry a dead man. In marriage, the suit and the shades will fall away, leaving behind a rotting corpse that will fill you with its stink. You will recognize him then for who he is. How can you ever forget the source of my creation? Marriage is out. You can keep your secret to yourself. Let me experience the bliss of ignorance. You will have your disappointment and your unending search for Third from the Left. But if I am to live in ignorance, then you will too. I will not let you in on Bhau's secret. The only way now to end the blockbuster Bollywood film that our life has turned into is to feed Bhau to his fire. What a surprise. I was so busy jabbering, I didn't realize I had reached the old crematorium.

Watchman enters.

WATCHMAN. Hey boy, what's up?

NANA. Who are you?

WATCHMAN. So did you manage to burn the old man? This place shut down the day your corpse turned up the last time.

NANA. Still trying to burn him. The corpse says he doesn't want to burn in the new place. If he has to burn, it will be here and nowhere else, he says.

WATCHMAN. That's a real cock-up. So, d'you want to burn him?

NANA. What's that?

WATCHMAN. I said, do you want to burn the corpse here, in the old place?

NANA. Come again?

WATCHMAN. I said, do you want to burn your old man's corpse in the old place here?

NANA. But how can . . .

WATCHMAN. This was a crematorium once, wasn't it? People kept coming and pleading with me night and day: Mr Watchman, can't we burn just this one? Won't you fulfill this last wish please? The crow will touch his rice ball and God will bless you. So, the boss and I decided: we'll burn corpses in black.

NANA. Black market for corpses!

WATCHMAN. Yup. Gets me some extra lolly and the crows their rice balls.

NANA. And the owner?

WATCHMAN. Sitting pretty. He gets his share. I'm waiting for an epidemic. I'll build a fancy house like nothing you've seen.

NANA. How much?

WATCHMAN. Two thousand. But let our market expand, the prices will come down.

NANA. Can't you do it for a little less?

WATCHMAN. Fixed rate, boss. It's a risky business. If there's a raid, the corpse gets confiscated.

NANA. So, when can I bring the corpse?

WATCHMAN. Any time you like. I'm always free.

NANA. Right. I'll be back as soon as I can arrange for the money.

WATCHMAN. No problem. (*Exit.*)

NANA. It's a matter of burning one body. Cost: two thousand. Where can I get that kind of money?

Voice off-stage: Hello, hello, hello. Can I come in? Can I come in?

NANA. Yes, sure. Who are you?

MAN. I'm LIC, LIC. The Life Insurance people.

NANA. Fuck! I'd clean forgotten. Bhau's life-insurance policy worth ten thousand. Hey, listen. I'm Bhau's heir.

MAN. I know, I know. Give.

(*Nana raises his hand to give him a high five.*)

Not high five. Not a high five. The policy. The policy.

(*Nana fetches the policy from the wings.*)

Here it is. Here it is. Your ten thousand. Your ten thousand. A cheque. A cheque.

NANA. Thanks. Hadn't expected it to come so quickly. By the way, why do you repeat everything twice over?

MAN. I repeat lines because there's no substitute for life insurance. I'm off. I'm off. (*Exit.*)

NANA. Balls! Ten thousand. Give us a break. Bhau, Bhau. (*Bhaurao enters*) Have you sobered up? Come, Bhau. It's all arranged.

BHAURAO. The wedding?

NANA. The burning. Come along. Off we go to your beloved old crematorium.

BHAURAO. What should I do with these clothes?

NANA. Take them along. Let's burn them. Come on. Quick. (*They go around the stage in circles. Then stop.*) Let's see your hand. I thought you'd lost it.

BHAURAO. What?

NANA. The fingertip I sewed on. Come (*They go round the stage again.*) Mr Watchman, here we are.

WATCHMAN. Got the corpse? Where is it?

NANA. That's him.

BHAURAO. Hello there.

WATCHMAN. This one's talking.

NANA. No, he isn't. Aural hallucination.

WATCHMAN. Oh, OK. Come along then. The pyre's ready. Put him on it.

BHAURAO. No.

NANA. Now what? Come on. Climb. It's the old crematorium. Don't be afraid. You didn't think this was for me, did you?

BHAURAO. Of course not. How could I?

WATCHMAN. Get up on it then.

Bhaurao stands in the centre of a platform.

BHAURAO. Bring on the logs.

Nana and the watchman mime building the pyre.

NANA. Here are the logs. Here are the cowdung cakes. Here's the black-market kerosene. Burn away in black. Our ways are parting, Bhau. Your body with all its breath and sensuous vitality will burn and turn into a dry bed of carbon and phosphorus. Burn, Bhau, burn to your heart's content.

You did not come on a bier. You walked to your pyre. Nana whom you leave behind will carry on the business of living with a capital of eight thousand in his pocket and a good-looking mother. Burn now, burn to your heart's content.

Take this log upon your chest. Make this sandalwood your pillow. Pull on a quilt of cowdung cakes. Burn, Bhau. Burn to your heart's content.

I will tell Mother that her Third from the Left died in an accident. Deceive Mother. Empty out her frame. Then perhaps she will see the First from the Left again. But you, Bhau. Burn bravely away.

Dear Mother, it's the truth. Third from the Left drowned in the river and died. Here are his suit and shades. To this Mother will say . . .

(*The stage darkens. Light on Ramaa.*)

. . . You're teasing me aren't you? I have seen the film. *Manoranjan* wasn't it?

(*Stage lights up again.*)

But you, Bhau. Burn away to your heart's content. You and Mother started me off. I must live the life you gave me. However hard I might want to, I'm not going to drown to death. Nor will I turn into Tarzan. For me there is no escape. You are departing. Lucky you. Yes, burn away, Bhau. Burn without regret.

WATCHMAN. Light her up.

NANA. With what?

WATCHMAN. Worry not, young man. We have a lighter.

Nana clicks the lighter to light Bhaurao's pyre. A red light suffuses him. A wild drum beat begins.

BHAURAO. Dear folks, wait a little while longer. There's still time for my skull to crack. Still time to finish my sermon. Circumstances are such that I must burn on the black market. But in the old crematorium still. That fills my heart with sacred satisfaction. Walking to this place has been like having a body massage. Like committing sati. My eyes feel cool under the dough. Behind the lids coloured glow-worms glow. It grows dark. I see strange shapes. I see something shaped like our chawl. I see Ramaa. I see the home she built. I also see her empty frame. Its sharp edge pierces me. I recall Nana. I recall the days before he came. I am now an outsider to it all. Breath makes the difference. I, who was so eager to burn from the moment I died, now recall an old story at the first touch of fire. (*In a raised declamatory voice*) The old woman is off on a pilgrimage. But she cannot bear to wrench herself away from home. Here she is instructing her daughter-in-law:

Listen to me, says the matriarch
Don't use up the milk and yogurt
On her way to Pandharpur
She has turned back from the border
Attend to what I say, my dear
My cracked bowl needs good care
The dung stack that I have made
Don't break it while I'm away
That vermicelli is for kheer
Don't touch its container
I worry so about my things
My grinding stone, pestle, mortar

> If a mendicant stops at our gate
> Say I'm on a pilgrimage

This mother-in-law who speaks of giving up the life of the world, declares pathetically at the end:

> Why should I go to Pandharpur
> What is there for me to see?
> My children and home are right here
> This is my Pandhari

However dear folks, my Pandharpur is not here. That home with its empty frame is not mine. If Ramaa sees another in her frame, so be it. After all, they do say, do they not, that Bandu Joshi is a spitting image of me. So let me say we are quits, and begin my journey into the unknown.

Silence.

NANA. Did you hear a sound?

WATCHMAN. No. It's not going to crack so soon. That must have been a log splitting.

BHAURAO. I have only one last wish. Although I have touched the rice ball, I must ask God for a boon. Nana is tired. He will have to have his ritual bath when he gets home. My prayer to God is this: let my skull crack before the water in our chawl is turned off. That is my only wish.

> Whether the body goes or stays back
> Before the water stops, let my skull crack.
> Whether the body goes or lingers
> I bow before thee, Lord Panduranga.

The drum beat grows louder. The light becomes redder.

NANA. The fire is blazing. Time for the skull to crack, Bhau. The flames frame a face. A young woman's face. She is probably sitting in the stalls, the seven-rupee or five-rupee row. Her seat is third from the left and I am destined to like her. But I see something else that is absolutely real. A fly sits with aplomb on the corner of the frame. She will not fly away till the curtain comes down. And I am not turning into Tarzan. Not just yet. So let me chant . . . Vitthal Vitthal, Jai Hari Vitthal.

BHAURAO. Nana Vitthal.

NANA. Bhau my Vitthal.

(*Drum beat grows even louder. Then stops. The drummers gather up their instruments. Before they slip them into their covers, one drummer slaps his tabla hard.*)

There it goes. I guess it has cracked.

WATCHMAN: Sure it has. You can't mistake that sound.

NANA. Cigarette?

GUARD. I smoke Green Thread–brand bidis.

NANA. Give.

The watchman hands Nana a bidi. Lights it with his lighter. Nana and the watchman walk off in opposite directions. Bhaurao stands still in the middle of the stage, his back turned to the audience. Intense red light. Silence. The curtain comes down.

THE END

SATISH ALEKAR INTERVIEWED BY REKHA INAMDAR-SANE

Edited and translated by Shanta Gokhale

You wrote Mahanirvan *25 years ago. Did you imagine then that it would have such a long life and be translated into more than half-a-dozen languages?*

Absolutely not. The play was first staged in its full form in 1974. I had written a shorter version of it a year or so earlier, at the request of Ram Patwardhan, editor of the Diwali Special issue of the weekly magazine *Mouj*. Since the play could not be accommodated in the issue because of its length, it came back to me. Theatre Academy was launched in 1973 on the terrace of my house in Shaniwar Peth, Pune. I had read my play *Mickey and Memsaab* in the playwrights' workshop organized by Satyadev Dubey in Pune in the summer of 1973. Theatre Academy decided to enter it for the State Drama Competition that year. When the 1974 competition came around, they wanted me to write another play for them. Since I had *Mahanirvan* with me, I began revising it and found it turning into a longer play. I don't know exactly how it happened, but in the end I had two acts, the first belonging to Bhau and the second to his son Nana. They were written in two different styles, though the play ended with a return to the first style. Had the play appeared in *Mouj*, it would not have become the play it is today.

I was 23 when I wrote it, and, to be honest, I didn't really care about its reception. It is entirely my good fortune that Theatre Academy has been staging it for over 25 years with practically the same cast.

Again, it is not as a result of my own efforts that the play has been translated into various languages. Looking back, it amazes me that a play we rehearsed for 25 days should have lived for over 25 years! Frankly, I am more interested in the production process than in how many shows a play manages to have. I love the whole business of getting a team together, rehearsing, organizing shows and experiencing firsthand the audience's response.

I must mention here a disaster that hit us when I was a schoolboy, a disaster with long-term effects. In 1961, the Panshet Dam burst and Pune city was flooded. There was water everywhere. It rose to over five feet in our house. Fortunately, this did not happen during the night, or the destruction would have been greater. It happened in broad daylight. Looking down from our terrace, I saw buildings collapse around us like so many houses of cards. When the water receded, it left behind mud that was four- to five-feet deep. The air was filled with the stink of rotting grain. The calamity took a toll on the old part of the city. It was time to redevelop the old neighbourhoods. An efficient plan for Pune's redevelopment had been drawn up by the able administrator Mr S. G. Barve. The municipal corporators of the time, across political parties, dynamited it. The development of the city was taken over by corporators and builders. As a result, Pune city grew into an extensive urban sprawl.

Water had entered our school. The wooden benches had rotted. The school became a shelter for people from the riverside slums. The teachers came together and organized a 10-day festival of plays on the school grounds to raise funds for relief. I was selected as a backstage volunteer. I saw all the plays from the wings. I was fascinated by the whole backstage world of grease paint, costumes, sets, dimmers and coloured filters.

The most popular annual event during our college days was the Purushottam Karandak drama competition. During my first year, I saw a production by B. J. Medical College of *Five Days*, a one-act play translated into Marathi by poet-playwright Sadanand Rege and directed by Jabbar Patel. With little by way of sets or lighting, and only a nominal use of drumming and war sounds, the small cast had managed to create, with skilful use of movement, gesture and expression, a totally convincing atmosphere of war. I found it very different from and more engaging than anything I had seen until then.

My eldest maternal uncle, Vitthal Gadgil was a senior lawyer, practising in Bombay High Court. He would visit Pune every weekend to meet his clients. The 17-room Gadgil-wada had gradually emptied after my grandfather passed away, and my aunts married and left for their marital homes. The family appointed me its sole caretaker. I lived there for six years, between 1965 and 1971. Every weekend, when my uncle came down to Pune, he brought with him a load of books, including playscripts, from the British Council library in Bombay. Recordings of plays were also available in the library. Uncle and I would listen to them together. I was astonished by how actors like John Gielgud, Richard Burton and Ralph Richardson could make such an expressive use of their voices without seeming to strain for effect. I was particularly affected by their voices at night when I listened to them alone in the vast spaces of the house.

One day when I was bored, I picked up John Mortimer's *The Judge* to read. I was so excited by it that I wrote my first one-act play, *Judge,* which I read out to my uncle that weekend. He was surprised. He said I had read well, pointed out a few small technical errors and predicted that I was going to be a playwright. A friend of mine, Samar Nakhate was then a student at the Film and Television Institute of India. He made a short film of the play, featuring the late Mohan Gokhale and head of the Maharashtriya Kalopasak theatre group, Rajabhau Natu. The play was published in the magazine *Manohar*, but I doubt if it was staged anywhere.

What were your earliest influences?

I was deeply influenced in my early years of writing/directing by Ritwik Ghatak's *Meghe Dhaka Tara*, Sombhu and Tripti Mitra's *Raja Oedipus* and *Putulkhela*, Vijay Tendulkar's *Shantata! Court Chalu Ahe*, Ebrahim Alkazi's National School of Drama productions *Threepenny Opera* and *Caucasian Chalk Circle* and Shanta Gandhi's play in Bhavai form, *Jasma Oden*. I am still affected by *Meghe Dhaka Tara*. In my opinion, it is a great film. I was so enthralled by its music that I used the Hamsadhwani composition 'Laagi lagan sakhi pati sang' in my first play, *Miki ani Memsahib*. Ravindra Sathe sang it.

Sombhu Mitra's *Raja Oedipus* was an unforgettable experience. He was staying at Hotel Pearl, across the road from Balgandharva Ranga Mandir. He ordered chicken before the show. He ate it distractedly, then walked across to the theatre. When he appeared on stage as Raja Oedipus, I could not recognize him as the dhoti-clad actor who had been eating chicken just a short while ago! I did not understand a word of Bengali, but the sound of his speech blew my mind. His command over his voice and the emotions he could summon with it reminded me of the plays I had heard in Burton's and Gielgud's voices. Every aspect of the play was imbued with Sombhu-da's perfectionism. The stage design, Tapas Sen's lighting design, the acting, all played together in harmony like an orchestral composition. I shall never forget Sombhu-da's performance. He was a thinker—he had thought deeply not only about theatre but also about life itself. That is why his plays told you, categorically, that theatre was not mere entertainment.

After that I saw plays produced by the National School of Drama. They emerged from a clearly conceived idea of theatre in which all elements—costume, acting style, set design—cohered to serve that ideal. Watching them, I realized what a great chasm separated actors like Naseeruddin Shah, Om Puri, Uttara Baokar and Manhar Singh from the actors on Maharashtra's professional and non-commercial stages. What made the difference was training. Although Marathi people are dedicated theatre-goers, there has been no theatre training here—the Marathi actor has always learnt on the job. That does not, cannot, happen with other performing arts. A musician must put in years of training with a guru before he performs. The same holds true for a dancer. But in theatre, anybody who shows talent can instantly call themselves an actor. The NSD plays demonstrated how important training was. Several attempts had been made in Pune to fill this lacuna. Jabbar Patel used to run a study circle and a 'journal club' in the Progressive Dramatic Association. Participants read Stanislavsky's *An Actor Prepares*, chapter by chapter. Theatre journals were borrowed from the British Council library and interesting articles from it chosen for reading together. We organized a series of three lectures by Dr Pramod Kale on the *Natyashastra*. His book, *The Theatric Universe* on the *Natyashastra* is considered a seminal work worldwide even today. When Girish Karnad was appointed director of the Film Institute, we heard him speak about Grotowski and his book, *Towards Poor Theatre*.

I found Brecht's idea of theatre to be diametrically opposed to Stanislavsky's. We saw his plays, but I found it difficult to enter them. I realized I could not own them in the way I could Sombhu Mitra's *Raja Oedipus*, although that was adapted from a foreign source and performed in a language I did not understand.

Not having had any formal training in theatre, I found it difficult to grasp theories of theatre. However, a chain of theatre thinkers, Stanislavsky, Brecht, Grotowski, was forming in my mind, and I became dimly aware that these were the chief thinkers of theatre. That a theatre practitioner could also be a thinker. That one could in fact speak analytically about the principles of theatre. This much I now understood. However, I could still not articulate ideas about theatre. Even today, I cannot analyse a play in a formal way. I am deeply respectful of those who can.

Setting theory aside, let us turn to practice. Before you wrote your first play—
the one-acter Jhulta Pool (*The Hanging Bridge*)—*you were not only doing*
backstage work for college productions but also acting. Can you say some-
thing about your experience of acting in Vijay Tendulkar's one-acter Ollakh
(*Acquaintance*)? *Did you feel that he had evolved a theatre language that*
was different from the generally practised?

No, I was quite blind back then. I did not feel easy with his lines, but could
not say so to anybody. The director was deep into improvisation. He was
talking about the form and content of the play; about the actor's bearing,
psychology, speech. He was throwing all these things at me, and I was
feeling stifled. My insides were turning over at the thought that perhaps I
had no clue as to what theatre was all about. The one-acter in itself was a
simple enough thing to do. 'He' and 'she' meet on a railway platform. They
do not know each other. They are only fellow passengers, both single. 'He'
tries to make her acquaintance, watching her closely all the while. 'She'
rejects his moves at first but soon recognizes a familiar middle-class angst
in him. They are both salaried employees. 'He' proposes marriage. 'She'
turns him down because she is the only breadwinner in her family. He
addresses her as 'Nirmal-Nima'. She calls him 'Madhu-Madhukar'. Ultimately their dream of marriage remains a dream. They go their own ways,
like trains running in different directions. All that remains is the sound
of trains rumbling over the tracks. The end. The play was published in
1957. We were rehearsing it in 1967, for the inter-collegiate Purushottam
Karandak drama competition.

My greatest problem was 'entering' the character of 'He'. I was not cut
out for that kind of thing. I found the dialogue tedious. There was nothing
theatrical there. The script was peppered with instructions that said 'Pause'.
'The pauses get filled by expression,' said the director. 'All you have to do
is enter the character. That will automatically determine the length of a
pause.' That is what the director thought I should do. What I actually did

was count in my head when the time came for a pause. There was also a point in the play where 'He' had to make a long speech:

> HE (*re-entering his reverie*). So I spotted you. The handbag on your shoulder was swinging because you had alighted in a hurry. A few strands of your hair blew in the monsoon breeze. You started walking slowly towards the station, keeping a firm hold on your umbrella. There was a grace in your walk. Many girls walk grace-fully, but with you it was different. You must have been extremely tired. Your step was heavy. But rather than marring your innate style, it enhanced it. I watched your back as you walked towards Boribunder, one hand holding up your rolled-up umbrella, the other holding up your sari a little to prevent the border from get-ting soiled in the slush. There was a wonderful rhythm in your every movement. I felt a powerful pull . . .

Each time I had to speak these lines, I'd wonder why the writer hadn't made the whole thing visual instead of describing it verbally in such minute detail. There was no drama there. Would the audience not find it boring? The entire thing struck me as very dull, but I didn't have the guts to say so out loud. I wondered later if the play had not been intended for the radio, and we were foisting it on a live audience. We won a prize but that gave me no satisfaction. I still felt a niggling regret. Mulling over it, I realized what we had given the audience was a half-baked world of sentiment—not a true theatrical experience, which should be like an unex-pected blow.

A more or less similar experience came my way the next year when we did Tendulkar's one-acter *Kallokh* (Darkness). But between the two lay a revelation—Tendulkar's full-length play *Shantata! Court Chalu Ahe* (*Silence! The Court Is In Session*) which had been entered for the State Drama Competition in 1967. I had seen a pre-competition show in Pune. This time I was encountering Tendulkar from the other side, as a viewer.

This show knocked down all my ideas about theatre. I experienced what was meant by the phrase 'watching with bated breath'. I still remember vividly the naive but earnest urge I felt to go up on stage and help poor Miss Benare. The emotional and social pain Miss Benare had to suffer as an unwed mother-to-be had seeped deep into our consciousness. Then came her last speech, sitting by a table, defeated, destroyed . . . The silence that fell on the house as the curtain dropped is a living memory.

I began to wonder how the same playwright could write three plays that were so different in form: *Shantata! Court Chalu Ahe, Ghashiram Kotwal* and *Sakharam Binder*. Why had I not been in tune with the same playwright's earlier plays even though I had acted in them? What is the process by which a writer's creativity develops? I must honestly confess I cannot answer these questions. I cannot even articulate exactly what I mean by being in tune with one play and out of tune with another.

Would I be right in saying that Tendulkar did not influence your writing?

If he did, I was not conscious of it. I cannot say: these are the plays I saw and here's their effect on my writing. I would describe his influence as something larger than style, form, expression. Here is a man who has been writing unstoppably for 40 years. His plays have permeated the very air we breathe. He has written few that have pleased the general public. Most of them stand apart from the popular plays of his times. It is these plays, realized through a variety of theatrical forms, that have filled the atmosphere in Maharashtra, and indeed the entire country, like stormy clouds. His plays have compelled viewers to face new forms and new themes. It is not easy to be a professional playwright for so long and still keep faith with your convictions every step of the way, never compromising them or bowing before public taste. Tendulkar's plays have become reference points in theatre. You are compelled to cite them in discussions about theatre. Playwrights like me have been able to write according to our instincts and convictions because he opened the way for us.

Your earliest plays were all one-acters. Can one say that Jhulta Pool *brought you prestige and fame?*

These things don't happen all of a sudden. In my case, years of appren-ticeship preceded *Jhulta Pool*. I had done backstage work for years, every-thing, right down to ironing costumes. I had also designed lighting. I had all this hands-on experience before I wrote my first play. *Jhulta Pool* wasn't the kind of success your question suggests. We were struggling to develop an audience for the productions we hoped to stage under the banner of our newly formed company, Theatre Academy. The group was created because senior members of our parent company, Progressive Dramatic Association (PDA), were supporters of the right-wing ideology of the Rashtriya Swayamsevak Sangh. Although PDA's head had gone along with us youngsters when we chose to do *Ghashiram Kotwal* under PDA's banner, the senior members couldn't stomach the idea. They saw the play as anti-Brahman whereas we were very excited by it. We were in our early twenties then. We wanted to continue with shows. A split was inevitable. PDA had a standing among Pune's audiences, but our new outfit had to create a space for itself. We performed *Jhulta Pool* and another one-acter as a double bill in people's homes, hoping naively that this audience that we were trying to cultivate would buy tickets for our public shows. The play they bought tickets to see was *Ghashiram Kotwal*.

You grew up in Shaniwar Peth in Pune's old town. You graduated from Fer-gusson College and went on to work at B. J. Medical College. In what way did these transitions affect you as a person?

The effect is reflected directly or indirectly in my plays. I worked in B. J. for 24 years, from 1972 to 1996. During these years, I became acutely aware of the poverty in our country. The dire poverty in Sassoon Hospital was levels below the economic conditions I'd seen in Shaniwar Peth. Every day, between 8 and 11 in the morning, some 3,000 or more patients would

attend the Out Patient Department alone. They still do. They were either
slumdwellers from Pune or from elsewhere, travelling anywhere up to
two days to get there. Some left their elders at the door of the hospital and
went away. I still remember those faces. Some new mothers were so poor,
they would abandon their newborns in the hospital and leave. Sassoon
gave free medical care. I watched the burden taking its toll, throwing the
infra-structure out of gear. The patients were so poor, they not only had
no money to pay for treatment, they couldn't even afford the form that
would admit them to the OPD. To top this, there was the terrible famine
of 1972 in Maharashtra which caused a huge exodus into Pune. That is
how the Sassoon Hospital OPD has been operating for over 135 years. I
had no direct contact with patients except when I took their blood sam-
ples. I would go away after that, feeling depressed. Nothing that I wrote
was ever going to reach these people. Even if a play of mine hit the jackpot,
these people would not be in the queue to buy tickets. Why write, then? I
introspected. I understood my limits. I decided to write only when an idea
pressured me to such an extent that I simply had to write. There was no
choice. I have kept my faith with that decision till today.

*Your work shows the deep connection you have with Pune. Could you talk
about that?*

There's a village or town in every writer's mind which reveals itself in his
writing either in realistic detail or in an exaggerated or imagined form.
Among the novelists, Shripad Narayan Pendse comes instantly to mind.
Details of space are as important as characters in fiction and realistic
drama. In other forms of drama, certain details might form their very
base. In *Jhulta Pool*, the presence of the river as the dividing line between
two economic classes is one example. The river bank, crematorium and
temple are central to *Mahanirvan*, and the wedding halls and Peshwe Park
of western Pune to *Shaniwar-Ravivar* (Saturday-Sunday). However, these

are not references to Pune as an objective space. They are parts of Pune that have taken root in my mind under various influences.

Broadly speaking, five of your plays including Begun Barve, Mahapur *and* Mahanirvan *could be described as fantasies. Fantasy appears to have a special fascination for you.*

I am often asked this question about fantasy. Nobody asks a realist playwright, 'What fascinates you about realism?' As for popular Hindi cinema, fantasy is accepted as a given. Let me give your question a shot. I saw my first plays from the wings. Perhaps that is why I grew up thinking that plays were a lie. Nothing in them is real. The living room is not a living room. The furniture is cheap and rented. The carpet is not a carpet at all. If that is so, why bother to display these things to the viewers? Let them have a direct view of the wings. Let the backdrop be a black curtain. Let them see that what they are watching is a staged play. Think of tamashas like *Gadhvache Lagna* (Donkey's wedding) and *Viccha Majhi Puri Kara* (Fulfill my desire). How economical their staging is. That's one thought.

The other thought is: our kind of plays are always going to be done on a tight or non-existent budget. The audience too will be thin. Why get involved with stuff like stage sets? The instruction with which *Jhulta Pool* begins is 'The stage is bare'. Economy of presentation entered my plays for these reasons and then went on to define them.

I must mention something else relating to fantasy. I am in the habit of going into reveries. I would be sitting in the canteen of B. J. Medical College. Some idea would drift into my mind, and I would drift away. My friend and colleague Dr Jayant Joshi would say, 'There goes Satish, woolgathering.' Why should this not happen to characters in a play? I believe anything can happen in a play at any time. A stage in an auditorium is an empty cube. In an outdoor performance, it is empty space. Characters can spring up at anytime and from anywhere. Why must they have reasons to enter or exit? They come and go because they are in a play and the play

cannot happen without them. It has always annoyed me to see characters
having tea or praying or changing clothes or cleaning vegetables or hand-
picking rice on stage. These things destroy my involvement with the play.
Also, instead of providing information about names and professions, why
not hand out the characters' biodata to the audience? How is such information relevant to a play as theatre?

Characters in *Mahanirvan* don't have surnames. Not a single resident
of the chawl is even given a first name. We do not know what any one of
them does for a living. In *Begum Barve*, characters, with the exception of
Shyamrao, have only surnames. Despite which the play is performed. A
play is what is given. The theme is important. Look at Tamasha—it starts
in one village, ends in another. Time is fluid. I decided, fairly early on,
to circumvent all the clutter and simply do theatre. You can call my plays
by any name—fantasy or any other. My aim is to engage the audience
completely without bowing an inch to their demands.

The exercise of writing a play has always been a challenge. A play
comes to me in its entirety. The dialogue comes complete with pauses,
vocal inflections, emotional flux. I write as a director. That is why, with
the exception of *Mahapur*, which was directed by the late Mohan Gokhale,
I have directed all my plays. This is not a sign of possessiveness—it is a
necessity. The empty spaces in my script are filled over the course of
rehearsals. You will see what I mean if you hear someone else reading my
play aloud and then me reading it aloud. Ultimately, though, the real
answer to why I write what and how I write is that I write as ideas come
to me, unpremeditated.

Your idea of a character strikes me as unusual. How do you think of them?

Generally, there are very few characters in my plays that are characters in
the conventional sense. I don't provide them with names, surnames, professions and back stories. The actor has to figure out what he must do as
a character. In the early days, actors would invariably ask me, 'Exactly

who am I?' My answer would be, 'You are an actor and you are acting in a play.' The protagonist of *Mahanirvan*, Bhaurao, has no history. He is a middle-aged man who has an attractive wife and a son. He dies suddenly. He lives in a chawl, but the stage is not set to look like one. He is not a keertan performer, but the instrument that accompanies keertans—a pair of castanets—is on the stage from the start. The actor who plays Bhaurao informs his wife Ramaa (and the audience) that he is dead in the play they are performing. Chandrakant Kale who played Bhaurao would keep in mind who he was as a person before becoming the actor playing Bhaurao. When he spoke to Ramaa, he would become 'Bhaurao'. Then become himself again while he listened to what the other actor was saying. When that actor finished, Kale would become 'Bhaurao' yet again and speak his lines. This might sound complicated, but Kale would manage it with great ease. Not in this play alone, but in *Begum Barve* too. There are times when he approaches his co-actors in a conventional way to speak his monologue emotionally (Act II: 'Do you call this new place a crematorium where you cannot lie on your pyre . . . '). Then he becomes an actor or the narrator who takes the play forward. He performs the actor/character tightrope act with utmost ease.

It takes great good fortune for a writer to find an actor who gets exactly what is written and then proceeds to underline every nuance with the precision of his performance. I have been the recipient of this great good fortune with our Theatre Academy actors. Who can forget the rice-ball scene performed by Ramesh Medhekar and Suresh Basaale? The chawl-dwellers Dileep Jogalekar, Uday Lagoo, Shreeram Pendse, and the actor who plays Nana, Prasad Purandare, all throw themselves into this celebration of theatre. Without them I am silenced. In this whole exercise, both actor and director must know exactly how much character the actor brings into play in any given scene. That is why, in this kind of theatre, it is very useful when the writer is also the director.

The creative process is a complex thing, I know. But do you start writing a play as soon as an idea grips your mind? What is their starting point ?

An idea strikes me and I write a play—that is not exactly how it happens. You might find the background to how I thought of *Mahanirvan* interesting. The crematorium next to the Omkareshwar temple was very close to our house in Shaniwar Peth. I grew up watching funeral processions going past our house every day. My mother's parents lived by themselves in their house. My grandfather was Vice-Chancellor of Pune University. One day, when there was nobody at home, my step-grandmother's sari caught fire while she was lighting the stove. She was badly burnt. She lay in Sassoon Hospital for eight or ten days. She didn't recover from her burns, and died. She was brought home from the hospital. That was the first funeral I watched at close quarters. Grandfather was extremely restless when the body was brought home. He wanted it cremated as soon as possible. 'Come on, hurry up,' he kept muttering in great distress. 'No need to tie the bier too tight. The crematorium is next door.' I couldn't understand why my grandfather, Pune's popular political leader and once a cabinet minister, Kakasaheb Gadgil, was talking in such a disturbed fashion at the age of 70. Grandmother was taken to Omkareshwar crematorium. Grandfather lit the pyre and finally calmed down. He sat on a nearby rock and said to somebody, 'See? She was burnt first, and then died. Fire took her in two instalments.' That remark stayed with me. The idea of this play came to me one day when I was mulling over that line. Later, Omkareshwar crematorium was closed down and a new one came up in Navi Peth.

It is said that the old crematorium was built after Chimaji Appa, the eighteenth-century war strategist of the Peshwas, was cremated on the Omkareshwar ground. Old residents of Pune would naturally expect to be cremated there, beside the river bank. One of them might easily insist that that is where he wanted to be cremated. Why not?

One more memory. Shaniwar Peth is full of wedding halls and temples. The Shaniwar Maruti festival was held in the summer every year, from Hanuman Jayanti to Akshay Tritiya. A keertan would be performed every night through those 15 days. I used to sleep on the terrace of our house. Whether I like to or not, I was forced to listen to the keertans that came at me through a screechy loudspeaker. Gradually I grew to rather like what I heard—well-known keertankars like Aphalebuwa, Neurgaonkarbuwa, Kopargaonkarbuwa. I absorbed the melodies, the beat and the narrative style of keertans. When I started writing *Mahanirvan,* I must have unconsciously decided that a dead man would not narrate his story in prose. As children, we are told the dead go to God. So his style would have to take a poetic form. The only poetic form of story-telling I knew was the keertan. That is perhaps why the first act and the last scene of *Mahanirvan* are written in keertan style. I say perhaps because, in 1971, when I wrote the play, I don't recall having thought consciously about any of this. Thinking about it now, I see what lies at its centre. I see its form. I also try to figure out, in my own way, what 'third from the left' might denote. People say the play is a black comedy. When I was writing it, I certainly wasn't saying to myself, 'I am writing a black or a white comedy.' I cannot comment usefully on what's called my 'oblique prose style and humour'. You could put it down to Pune culture, where people never say anything straight.

When you have finished writing a play, do you read it out to people? Do you use their suggestions to make changes in the script?

Yes, I do read my plays out to people. Readings give me a clue to how the audience will respond to them. It is also a kind of pre-preparation for directing a play. I find these readings extremely useful. I normally do them informally before a bunch of Theatre Academy actors. But I don't make changes in the script. The changes or refinements happen during rehearsals. There are small differences between the published script of *Mahanirvan* and the performance script that we have evolved. Some

passages and lines from the published script have been dropped. The
women characters too have been dropped. Otherwise, no changes have
been made. I write a play only when I am able to 'see' it.

Mahanirvan *is structurally disjointed—there is no coherence between the*
first and second acts. People have said that the second takes the play away
from its theme. Did you write only Act One first? When did you write the
line 'at least drop the curtain on Act One'?

As I said earlier, I wrote the play first as a long one-acter. When we decided
to enter it for the competition, it was expanded into two acts. This doesn't
mean that I simply added a second act onto the first. In the process of
expanding the play, I split the original long one-acter into two, and rewrote
the whole thing. This is a play within a play. That is the essence of the traditional keertan. Even as the performer is presenting his sermon, he slips
into observations about the contemporary social or political situation,
indicating thereby that he is presenting a play. I have put this form to my
own use. Act Two also presents a play. Nana too is performing his kind of
keertan. I don't agree that the structure is disjointed. The narrator of Act
One is Bhau and of Act Two, Nana. The generational difference between
them is reflected in the structure. If you take the structure of the play as a
whole, it begins in keertan style and ends in keertan style, thus completing
the circle. The narrators of the two acts are bound to have different styles
of narration. Whenever we have performed this play exclusively for a
young audience, we have received a warmer response to the second act.

Mahanirvan *is seen as an object lesson in absurdist theatre. Where does*
your sense of the absurd come from? From your reading of Western literature
or from personal experience?

I first became aware of this thing called absurdist theatre when I read
Dr Kumud Mehta's essay, 'Has the Absurd Invaded Indian Theatre?' In it,
she had compared the chawl residents of P. L. Deshpande's revue-type play
Batatyachi Chaal with the chawl residents in *Mahanirvan*. When I was

writing it, I wasn't aware that I was writing an absurdist play. I don't believe even today that it is an absurdist play. There is no lack of logic in its theme. It is not about the meaninglessness of life. I think life is really the absurd thing, not my play. Nowadays, during funerals in crematoria, priests have been replaced by recordings of the last rites. How absurd is that? I have noticed that any playwright or director who abandons realism to create his own theatre language is labelled illogical and therefore absurdist. Being ignorant of the literary definition of absurdism, this is all I can say.

How satisfactory have you found the productions of your plays in other languages?

To be quite truthful, I feel the play is mine only in the Marathi productions that I direct. Not that I haven't responded to productions in other languages. I saw a Hindi *Mahanirvan* directed by Alakh Nandan in which B. V. Karanth played the main role. He caught the exact tone of the keertan using the Braj dialect. My problem with other languages is that I miss the visceral connection I have with Marathi. The Bharat Bhavan Hindi version I saw included women among the chawl-dwellers. It was an engaging production. The Gujarati version *Tathaiyya*, directed by young Mumbai-based director Mahendra Joshi, was a different experience altogether. It was a wild production. He used something akin to Bhavai in place of the keertan form. When Bhaurao came down from the loft, it was from the flies. An effective use was made of Gujarati folk music. The general atmosphere was energetic and lively. You could see the director's individual stamp on the production, yet the play did not stray away from the theme. The production did over a hundred shows. I attended the fiftieth. Most unfortunately, Mahendra Joshi died prematurely. A thinker-director who had the potential to give Gujarati theatre a new direction died of a sudden heart attack.

I saw another production of a very different kind in Bengali, directed by Sohag Sen. She listened to a recording of the Marathi production and created her own script with the help of the English translation. She did not use Veena Alaase's Bengali translation. Sohag incorporated Bengali death rituals in the play without departing from the theme. She even did one show of this production in Pune.

I saw another Hindi production recently in Delhi, directed by Roysten Abel. He called it *Azaadi ek Laash ki* (The liberation of a corpse). He used the original play to then take off into a world of his own creation. He used a band with a drum set, guitar, trumpet and saxophone and beautifully choreographed movements. His chawl residents danced and sang as a chorus. The funeral procession was choreographed. His crematorium had been taken over by Pepsi, the priest wore the Pepsi logo as the sacred mark on his forehead. Lyrics had been specially composed to fit various situations. The music by Piyush Mishra had a great beat. It was an energetic production which reflected the distinctive style and vision of the director. I enjoyed watching it. The second act was quite different from the original. The old crematorium was turned into a haunt for homosexuals. Habib Tanvir was sitting beside me. He had seen the production in which Karanth had acted. He was very restless. People who had seen the Marathi production found this one unappealing. But I enjoyed it. I grant directors the right to use a written script merely as a crutch to lean on. If the director has vision, he can carve out new directions with his experiments.

Your two most important plays are Mahanirvan *and* Begum Barve. *In both, music, albeit from two different streams of Maharashtra's musical tradition, plays a significant role. However, you do not draw on folk literature for your narrative material as do playwrights like Girish Karnad.*

I love many things about our old theatre. Music is one of them. Although I have seen only one of the old music plays, *Saubhadra*, the old stage music is still alive. Even today I only have to hear a few notes of those hits and I am instantly transported to the old Sangeet Natak world. I hear the organ playing. There's so much theatricality in the organ. When I was writing *Begum Barve*, I didn't have to look for references. If the scene I was writing called for a stage song, it came unbidden. The spoken Marathi of those days, the early 1900s, the golden era of the Sangeet Natak, also came quite naturally to me.

I have already talked about how I became acquainted with keertans and began to enjoy them. Another form of music I loved for its sound was wedding brass bands. I loved not only the sound but also the players' costumes that signified their level of professional success. This was before synthesizers invaded the scene. When I use elements of tradition, I do so out of the love I have for them. That's true also of the keertan in *Maha-nirvan*. I am often ironic in the way I use them, but my irony is lined with love. You create something new only when you use tradition with respect and understanding.

Unfortunately, this was not true of the wave of plays that broke on the Marathi stage during the eighties after the success of Tendulkar's *Ghashiram Kotwal* and Karnad's *Hayavadana*. Neither play had used the elements of folk theatre as a gimmick. What happened later, when the Sangeet Natak Akademi launched the Young Directors' Assistance Programme, was a rash of plays in which folk elements were forcibly thrust into urban plays. The only exceptions were Ratan Thiyam's *Chakravyuha*, Bhanu Bharati's *Pashu Gayatri* and Vaman Kendre's *Zulva*. The others had used folk elements merely to fulfil the terms of the assistance programme during its first five years which stipulated that only directors who used folk elements in their productions would receive funds. Mahesh Elkunchwar and I were on the Sangeet Natak Akademi committee. We insisted that the condition be removed. Finally, it was.

Throughout this time, you had a group of talented actors at hand—members of the Theatre Academy. You had a singer-actor of the calibre of Chandrakant Kale. Would Mahanirvan and Begun Barve have been as successful as they are without him?

We in Theatre Academy were all more or less of the same age. None of us was a trained actor. We were learning on the job with every play we did. I had just begun to write. Anand Modak composed his first music for *Mahanirvan*. We were evolving as we struggled. That I had someone like Chandrakant Kale in my plays was a stroke of sheer good luck. He is one of India's finest singer-actors. I am not the only one who thinks so. G. P. Deshpande has gone on record to say so in one of his essays.

Besides your own work, you led a Ford Foundation–funded playwrights'-workshop project. How did this project and funding come about?

When I returned from our international tour of *Ghashiram Kotwal* in 1980, I submitted a playwrights' workshop project to the Maharashtra State Literary Culture Corporation. The corporation did not as much as acknowledge it. I sent them reminders, but continued to draw a blank. Sometime in 1982–83, I received a letter from the Ford Foundation to say that they would like to offer financial assistance for work on contemporary art expressions; and that if I had a suitable proposal, they would be happy to look at it. I was surprised, because Ford Foundation only supported traditional art forms. The change in policy came about because of two women—Ford Foundation Programme Executive Pushpa Sundar (nee Bansode from Nagpur), and director of the National Centre for the Performing Arts, Dr Kumud Mehta. These two women convinced the Ford Foundation's New York Office of the need to change their financial-assistance policy. Their argument was that a new generation of creative writers, born around the time of Independence, had now come of age. It was the demand of the times that if the state could not support this contemporary work, organizations like the Ford Foundation should take note of it. It was through Kumud Mehta's efforts that Dalit writers Daya Pawar and Laxman Mane received funding. The Indian National Theatre were the next beneficiaries, then Pune's Dalit theatre, then Granthali, the readers' movement. This chain stretched into 1995, at which point Ford Foundation changed its policy once again and began to support Adivasi art and concentrate on the media.

When I received the letter from Ford Foundation, I sent them the proposal I had written for the State Literary Corporation. Pushpa Sundar came down to Pune and explained to me how a proposal was to be written. I resubmitted the rewritten proposal for what came to be called the Playwrights Development Scheme. The Centre took almost three years to sanction the funding because, although we would get the money in Indian currency, it would come into the country in American currency and so fell under the Foreign Funding Regulation Act. The project, which spanned three years from 1985 to 1987, was a huge success. Twelve new playwrights participated. Six plays were produced. Four were published. The members of the Theatre Academy threw themselves headlong into the work. Vijay Tendulkar agreed to be the advisor. I used to work the whole day at my job and then start the project work, which included filing reports. We had no paid full-time assistance. Nandu Pol and Suresh Basaale looked after office work.

When the project wound up, we did not apply for a second grant although there was a possibility it would have been sanctioned. For one thing, the work had put an unbearable strain on us. For another, we didn't want to become dependent on external funding.

We submitted our second proposal later, around 1989, for what came to be called the Regional Theatre Group Development Project. The idea was to develop well-funded centres for theatre in places where theatre was already a strong presence, thanks to local groups and patronage. The idea was inspired by New York's Theatre Communication Group (TCG).

This is a network of some 500 plus groups spread across America and running on a no-profit-no-loss principle to produce professional plays. When I was on an Asian Cultural Council Rockefeller Fellowship in 1984, I spent an entire day in the TCG office in New York. It had struck me then that we could create a similar network of theatre groups in Maharashtra. My proposal was sanctioned. We developed four centres— Kankavali, Kolhapur, Satara and Solapur. One hundred and five shows of off-mainstream plays from Pune and Mumbai were staged in these centres over the next three years. The centres themselves hosted each other's plays. The group in Kankavali launched an annual theatre festival for off-beat plays which continues to this day. Chandrakant Kale and Shrikant Gadre helped organize the first one. Pratyaya, the Kolhapur group, staged a magnificent production of *Raja Lear*, poet Vinda Karandikar's adaptation of Shakespeare's tragedy. Dr Sharad Bhutadia directed it and played the lead role. For six years, the theatre scene in Maharashtra bubbled with excitement. I did all the work required for the project, from writing the initial proposal to drawing up schedules to writing and submitting regular reports. Mohan Agashe, Jabbar Patel and Nandu Pol were a huge help. Our theatre projects came to an end in 1996.

That is when you took over as the director of Lalit Kala Kendra, the performing arts department of the University of Pune. What made you decide to change jobs?

I had begun to find my work as a biochemist at B. J. Medical College dreary. It being a government-run institution, I had a chance to take voluntary retirement at the end of 20 years of service. I was seriously considering retiring when two things happened. Kirti Jain, director of the National School of Drama, was coming to the end of her term. The Culture Ministry was on the lookout for a new director. I was a member of NSD's Academic Council. The Ministry asked me if I would take over the directorship. Meanwhile a long-delayed sanction for the post of professor at

Pune University's performing arts department had finally arrived. The Vice-Chancellor, Dr Shridhar Gupte was eager for me to take it up. I wasn't keen on going to Delhi. The NSD already had a well-oiled system in place and a large budget outlay. Rather than go there merely to continue doing what had been done, I preferred the idea of starting full-time training for students of the performing arts in a place where such training did not exist. Creating something out of nothing was a bigger challenge.

Around that time, Theatre Academy too had arrived at a point of stagnation with no further growth in view. I thought seriously about my choices and rejected the Delhi offer in favour of the post at Pune University. In the last three and a half years, I have concentrated on developing and administering syllabi for dance, music and theatre. What I've managed to do is there for all to see. Before I quit, I hope to bring the Lalit Kala Kendra to a point of development from where there will be no looking back. I'll see what I can do after my term ends.

I have come this far because of the help I have received from leading people in the fields of dance, music and theatre. Those who have played crucial roles in the development of the Lalit Kala Kendra include, from music and dance, Pandit Bhimsen Joshi, Pandit Suresh Talwalkar, Pandita Veena Sahasrabuddhe, Samar Nakhate, Vikas Kashalkar, Rohini Bhate, Sucheta Bhide-Chapekar; and from theatre, Dr Rajeev Naik, Vaman Kendre, Vijay Kenkre, Chandrakant Kulkarni, Shyam Manohar, Mohan Agashe and the architect couple Nachiket and Jayoo Patwardhan. Mahesh Elkunchwar has been a regular external lecturer. Vijaya Mehta and Vijay Tendulkar have also visited. And there's the support I have received from my colleagues, Shubhangi Bahulikar and Praveen Bhole.

And now the last question. Do you find that being part of the establishment with the stress of administrative work and advancing age, has weakened your ability to think of new ideas?

I am about to complete *Pidhijaat* (Dynasts). I could never write plays as a discipline or routine anyway. The interesting part of theatre for me has always been rehearsals, running shows and facing the audience. For my kind of theatre, I need organizational support and an assured platform. Like Girish Karnad, I am not a prolific playwright. After *Hayavadana* (1971), his next important play was *Nagamandala* (1988). Vasant Kanetkar and Vijay Tendulkar have written 30 to 40 plays each while others have written fewer. I have written only when an idea has pushed me to writing. It is the same today. But while I wait for an idea to come to me in its own time, my earlier plays continue to have reruns. The administrative work I do goes towards helping others create art. It gives me great joy to be witness to the artistic development of the young generation.

*

Mahanirvan was originally produced by the Theatre Academy and first performed on 22 November 1974 at Bharat Natya Mandir, Pune. The production was closed after over 400 shows. In 2018, Natak Company, Pune, invited Alekar to direct a revival. The cast for that production was entirely new, but the original musical score by late Anand Modak was retained. Despite the restrictions on theatre activity during the Covid-19 pandemic, the production has completed 40 shows and is still running.

A CONVERSATION WITH DOLLY

Thakishi Samvad

Translated by Shanta Gokhale

CHARACTERS

OLD MAN

DOLLY

On stage are the following: an old-fashioned work desk with a table lamp, laptop and books, an old sewing machine and wheelchair half-visible from the wings and dozens of Amazon cartons scattered around. An old man of 75/80 rummages through one of them. It contains a bedpan, urine pot and other such items.

OLD MAN (*speaking softly*). You're fed up sitting at home, aren't you? Or you've begun to realize you are fed up. But what does being fed up mean? How has this long solitude affected me? As well as not knowing how long it'll last. Namaskar. These are tough days. I am Suresh or Ramesh or Bhaurao or Nanasaheb. I'm not particular about names. Call me anything. Old man, grandpa, uncle. I'm old enough. Past 75, not a day less. Living alone with all sorts of memories—facts, alt-facts, things that happened, were made to happen, personal, social, political—the lot. Where do I stand in all this? What do I have to say? More fundamentally, do I or do I not have something to say? Do I or do I not have a position on this solitude that's been imposed on us? Have I decided not to take it? Am I scared to take it? Is somebody scaring me off from taking it?

(*Pause*)

See what powerful questions this solitude has set off? There are questions. Persistent doubts. These things happening in the outside world—are they real? What's going on inside me—is that real? Or is somebody screwing us? I know, I know. Screwing isn't a word that goes with my age. But let it pass. Put it down to senility.

But why hasn't she come yet?

(*Pause*)

I bet you're wondering who this *she* is? (*Laughs*) No, not my wife. Girlfriend, beloved? Not that either. And certainly not democracy, equality, mental clarity. Who is she, then? I stand here alone like an old-style stage narrator. So you think she has to be the actress who always enters late? You think wrong. We are not in a play. You are witness to all that is happening here. Between you and me, acting is not my strongest suit. Have a little patience. You'll soon see her. Dolly will come. At least she should. With me in quarantine, she really must. Soon.

(*Pause*)

Sometimes I wish the third bell would ring out loud and clear, the curtain would lift and the past would appear as it was. Bells are funny things. We hear temple bells and church bells. Mosques don't have bells but they have the azaan at regular times. These public sounds are the background score to our private lives. But we hardly notice them. The bell that you hear most clearly as something rung specially for you is as the paying public in the theatre. (*Startled*) There I go. Still talking about the theatre. Old habits die hard. Anyway, now that I have blurted it out, let me at least make an applause-worthy speech. You aren't compelled to clap. I was half-joking. So dear people, this is our time between birth and death. We are on this planet because right now there's nowhere else for us to be. Coming to the bell. The theatre has already been mentioned earlier. Now, listen. I'm about to give my speech:

'Although everybody can hear the third bell that heralds the start of a play, the bell that heralds a baby's entry is heard only by the mother who gives it birth, and the bell that heralds the final exit is heard only by the one who is dying.'

(*Listening to himself critically.*)

No. That hasn't worked. Let me refine it a bit. Listen to this:

'Although all can hear the bell that tolls the start of a play, only the mother-to-be hears the bell that tolls her baby's birth, and only the one drawing his last breath hears the bell that tolls his death.' You are welcome to keep either version. Or both. Or neither. It makes no difference. Nothing makes any difference nowadays. I'm telling you . . . the very shape of our existence has become warped. Is it because of the lockdown or did it never have a shape? What, then? What are we supposed to do with ourselves? Is the very idea of living that we cherished in our minds slipping away through our fingers like sand? And these hands, constantly wet with washing, are allowing it to happen, leaving some sticking to them. A case of winning the fort but losing the brave heart who won it. (*Somewhat dramatically.*) In the course of this long and enforced solitude, the false glitter of the firmament has faded away like air from a puncture, revealing to us the entirety of the natural world. The Himalayas, never before visible from this house, may now be seen clearly from the terrace. The space of our innate arrogance having been squeezed with this confinement to the solitude of our homes, the peacocks from the woods behind have begun to strut into our gated spaces, plumage proudly fanned out, cocking a snook at the security guards. Pairs of coucals which we could never spot before now perch regularly on our dense green colony trees.

(*Pause*)

So? What do you say to that speech? Eh? It's all very amusing. I said a while ago that you are witness to all that is happening here. But to tell you the truth, I'm not even sure you are here. You've always kept your distance from the kind of theatre we do. Now social distancing is the rule. I have no idea whether you are here or not here . . . or whether this show is being streamed online. Things are all mixed up. For my part, I've assumed I am conducting this conversation . . . it is a conversation . . . alone. See, we need to have some amusement. How much time do I have? Don't I need some entertainment to amuse myself?

Now a bit of speculation. Until Dolly arrives.

Entertainment? What is that? Dance, music—meaning, art? Which fucker . . . sorry: esteemed personage, has decreed that you must turn to art if you're looking for entertainment? Even the games our minds play can be entertaining. In fact, they are more entertaining than anything else. You are your own master. There is an old saying. 'You are the instrument and you the player.' You and your mind. You're free to play what games you please. With art, you land up with the problem of grading. Charles Chaplin or Laurel and Hardy? Who is to decide? Those who are entertained by them or some others? Since we are talking about entertainment, here's the question that has always bothered me. Do we define entertainment as anything that pleases us? Or do we decide that only that which pleases us is entertainment? What exactly happens when we are amused or find a way to pass the time? Or are we to understand that temporarily forgetting a part of our existence and being pleased are different and independent of each other? What is the precise zone that entertainment occupies? Red, orange, green? And who decides which? One thing is reassuring. Once a lockdown is relaxed, the liquor shops in all three zones will throw their doors open. That's enough for ordinary people like me. But what about the big guns of the world? What entertains them? Say some big gun says: heck, I'm bored. What, then? When I say big gun, I'm thinking Alexander the Great who visited India in some year BCE. How did Alexander entertain himself in those ancient times? Get up each morning and march with his cavalry into some unknown place? Get up each morning and conquer a new place? Some of his womenfolk stayed back. Some of our womenfolk went with him to Greece. Leave some womenfolk behind permanently in different places and take women from these places by force or of their free will to board and bed with, mixing breeds from all over . . . could that itself have been Alexander's entertainment? And what about Cyrus the Great who came from Persia or Iran to India even before Alexander. What entertained him? Feeding us dates? Or injecting words from his language into ours?

(*Pause*)

Perhaps you think this is going too far back to discover the meaning of entertainment. But you'll see how these references will gradually creep forward and come right up to our times, that is, beyond 2014 right up to where we are now. I am not referring to the big guns alive today or recently dead like Pramod Mahajan, Gopinath Munde, Amit Shah and so forth. Certainly not. Why put your finger in Maruti's navel? I'm too old for that. What if I'm screwed as an urban naxal? I'll have to go bawling to a lawyer. I'm too old for that. Instead, let me chill in this enforced solitude. Let me make a presentation to you, in this lockdown that has come at the tail end of my life, of the research I have been doing quietly and committedly for years, not at anybody's bidding but as a personal mission. With Dolly's help. But where is she? Where are you, Dolly? We've completed 60 years this year, my girl.

Dolly enters. She is fortyish. Neat as a pin. A little impersonal. Body language charmingly feminine. It is a bonus if she can sing. Her hairdo and dressing style are traditional. But she need not stick to one costume. Her general demeanour should create a doubt about whether she is a real person or something else.

DOLLY. Here I am, master. And what's this about completing 60 years? You turned 60 eons ago. You're not cheating about your age, are you? It's time for your 80th-year celebration. Your mother was alive to bless you with an aarti when you completed 60. If you manage to make it to 80 without a ventilator, I'll be there to do the honours, master.

(*She straightens her pallu and addresses the audience.*) How's that? A blast of an entry, right? Time for a meaningless announcement, followed by a song.

Airline announcement: 'The captain has switched off the seatbelt sign', etc., followed by 'Mangal desha, Pavitra desha' [Blest terrain, sacred terrain, the terrain of Maharashtra, I bow before you].[1]

Suitable visuals could be projected on the screen to accompany the song.

OLD MAN. Dolly, we are 60 years. Not me. Our Maharashtra. And you chose to sing about just that. Attagirl. Poet Govindagraj wrote that song.

DOLLY (*to the audience*). That's the poet and playwright whose statue was vandalized in Pune in 2017. He wrote poetry as Govindagraj and plays in his real name, Ram Ganesh Gadkari. He died in 1919. He was only 34. His statue lived a while longer than him. His plays are with us even today, permanently alive. Those who vandalized his statue were publicly honoured. Spanish flu was his lot in 1919. COVID-19 is ours in 2020. We must say one thing about COVID-19: it doesn't discriminate between castes, genders, religions, the rich and the poor or those who vandalize statues and those who don't.

OLD MAN (*holding an enamel urine pot taken from its Amazon box*). Dolly, since you have been talking about Gadkari, it follows that we should talk about the other side of the Marathi theatre coin: Diwakar. There is a personal anecdote about the two which I'm going to narrate later. (*Dolly has been watching his movements closely. She walks up to him. He waves the urine pot in the air.*) Time for my prostate break.

DOLLY (*in a low voice*). Don't throw it away. We've been told to measure it.

OLD MAN. Woman, let me pass some first before we talk of measuring. (*Exit*)

---

1 Available at https://ytube.io/3ZYn.

DOLLY. Let's do Diwakar during master's physical break. Real name Shankar Kashinath Garge. Writer of dramatic monologues. Gadkari's contemporary. Born 1889. Died 1931. Lived in Pune's Shaniwar Peth. Gadkari lived in Kasba Peth. Gadkari's plays of five acts, sometimes six, were full of long, resounding speeches and songs, sung by singer-actors like Balgandharva. But then there was also *Mooknayak*, a two-and-a-half page playlet in which the hero does not say a single word. Gadkari became a name. Diwakar did not. He was just an ordinary salary-earning teacher in Nutan Marathi Vidyalaya. His writing did not go beyond a paragraph here, a half-page there, two pages elsewhere. But both men admired Shakespeare. Master says they were bosom pals. (*Softly*) Perhaps he bluffs, who knows? OK. That's enough. I'm not teaching theatre history here.

(*Listens. A baby is crying in one of the Amazon boxes. Dolly approaches the carton, bends down, lifts out a baby and then begins a Diwakar monologue.*)

Hush, little one. Now who was it who called you darkie? Tell them I'm not a darkie. Look at me. Fair as fair can be. We'll make our Chingi a necklace. And a pendant. And armlets and anklets. We'll dress her in a long skirt and blouse and off she'll go, mincing her way to school. My little one is going to grow into a clever girl. She's going to read big books. Then our Soni will be married. Soni, hey Soni, how should your husband be? Dark or fair? Dark? Never. Our Soni will marry a husband as bright as a star. I'll give her such a wedding, such a wedding as you have never seen before. I'll give a dowry of a thousand rupees. A full thousand. There will be drums and pipes and trumpets—an entire band. And the wedding procession? My oh my! Such dazzling fireworks. Fountains and pinwheels and zooming rockets. They'll light up the sky. But Chingi, I hope you're not going to quarrel. If you do, watch out. You must keep your husband in your fist. Your marriage must stand out as the ideal. And let me tell you, your first baby must be born here. The others can come in your home. She is fortune's child, my Chingi. She will mother many children. But tell me, would you like to have daughters or sons? Girls? Perish the thought. Don't get into that mess. Our Chingi will have son after son. And a horse carriage and rich clothes. She will not want for anything. But there's time for all that. Don't start preening yourself just yet, little one. Look at her showing off. Puffing up with pride. Just look at her. What is that you are saying?

(*Pause*)

The lockdown? Of course, it will end. Sooner rather than later, I'm sure. But, Chingi dear, I get the feeling you are going to grow up online now.

(*Returns to the carton from which she picked up the quilt that she converted into the baby. She unfolds the quilt. Wrapped in it is a PPE set— an N-95 mask, gloves, etc., all of which she puts back in the carton.*)

So that was Diwakar. Did the master tell you anything? No? Nothing? I mean about himself? Like where he is from, his family. Amazing. What kind of character is he? Look at Gadkari's characters. Or Diwakar's. But who's to tell him? Between you and me . . . Are you there? Or are we on Zoom or something? I don't know what's going on here. I just wanted to say I've been with the master since 2014. I joined, and up there the Congress fell and a new power took over. But the master was unmoved. Said nothing, revealed no values of his own, took no position. Nothing. No way of knowing what he thought. I've heard he was an activist in his youth when Emergency was declared in 1975. His father was imprisoned in 1942. But after 2014, since I came to serve him, he's been deftly flipping sides, sometimes right, sometimes left. The aim is always not to hurt anybody. Someone says something for the government, he nods his approval. Someone says something against the government, he nods his approval. It's like acknowledging a singer's skill in arriving on the first beat spot on. Should a man not have an independent opinion? Admitted, he's no longer a spring chicken. His spine is bent with age as it is. When I said that to the master once, guess what he told me? As a boy, he used to bend to touch his father's feet after he had recited his tables. His father would stroke his back and box it lightly saying, 'Just fight.' Once his father was angry with him because he hadn't studied hard enough. He boxed his back hard, shouted, 'Just fight' out of habit. The master writhed in pain and ended up, he said, with a chronic back ache. So, if his spine is bent now, it could be because of age or the blows on the back. You can never tell with a human spine. Is it originally bent or have circumstances bent it? Or does the man with the bent spine think it is straight? Let me tell you. I have not found out the master's full name to date. But, somehow, these parcels seem to find him. (*Pulls out an oximeter and mask from one of them*) See? We're all set. We've even got a wheelchair. He's not showing any signs yet. We've only just started this conversation. But you don't get advance notice for such things. Considering his age, it's best to be prepared, don't you think? Temperature gun, PPE, all the props are here. It's part of our practice. When a prop is shown, you must use it before the end. Habits die hard. (*As she tidies up the stuff in the cartons*) He did not marry. Nobody knows why. It's like knickers. Whether you take them off or not, they are yours. Your decision. Who are we to question it? What did he do before 2014? Did he have a job? His father owned a small bookshop. In the old town. He sold second-hand school books. That sort of thing doesn't earn you much. His mother died after the master completed 60. He mentioned once, maybe twice, that her family had given her a lot of jewellery. That's all I know about this character. I don't ask questions. Why poke one's nose where it doesn't belong? I know he is constantly immersed in his research. But what is this research about? Is it theoretical or practical? Since when has he been doing it? Is he really doing research or is it a delusion? Or is he fibbing? Who is funding the research? Is it someone here or abroad? Or is he funding himself? (*Puts on mask and gloves*) Does he have an NGO, a not-for-profit outfit? Has he published his research or has he still not arrived at his findings? Basic question. Why is he doing research? We'll find out soon. Gosh! Urine! (*Shouts*) Master, don't throw it away. I'm coming. (*Exit*)

Lights dim and focus on the Amazon cartons. Flight announcement on the soundtrack: 'The captain has switched off the fasten seatbelts sign,' etc., ending with 'Smoking is prohibited in the lavatories.'

The announcement fades. The song 'Dole he julmi gade' begins to play and a Whatsapp message appears on the screen:

This song was written by B. R. Tambe. They say he wrote it in 1932 but composer Vasant Prabhu set it to music much later, around 1960. The story goes that, one afternoon, Vasantrao was glancing through Tambe's poems. One poem in particular brought tears to his eyes. He took off his glasses, wiped his eyes and put them back on. When he turned the page, it was to this poem, 'My beloved, there's magic in your eyes, don't gaze at me so'. The tune came to him even as he was reading it.[2]

The song fades. The old man enters. He is now wearing a scarf.

OLD MAN. So, Ram Ganesh Gadkari lived in Kasba Peth. In the evening, when he was tired of writing, he would walk down to Mehunpura in Shaniwar Peth, stop by at the Vartak snuff shop, buy himself a small packet, take a turn at Veer Maruti and head towards the Omkareshwar temple. Diwakar would be standing at the corner of Tambe Lane. He lived nearby in Bapatwadi. The two would then walk towards the Mutha river, either to the Patwardhan tomb or the Omkareshwar

---

2 Available at https://ytube.io/3ZYo

music house, chatting all the way. When the mood took him, Gadkari would come with a fishing rod on his shoulder and the two would sit angling by the Mutha river. Diwakar was vegetarian while Gadkari loved his fish. We were talking a while ago about what entertained big guns. Nonstop conversation accompanied by a pinch of Vartak's snuff entertained these two most. There's a story about them. The year was 1918. The Spanish flu epidemic was raging. Quarantine rules were in force. Gadkari had an inkling that things were not well with him. He was constantly ill. He used to be terrified, nobody knew why. On this day, Gadkari was particularly anxious. He looked deeply disturbed. Diwakar said to him . . .

DOLLY (*playing Diwakar*). You're silent today, master.

OLD MAN (*playing Gadkari*). All is not well with me, Shankar Kashinath . . . here, take a pinch. (*Holds out a packet of snuff.*)

DOLLY. Why do you say that? Has the fever not left you yet?

OLD MAN. It is mild. But it is there every day. Comes at sunset, leaves at sunrise.

DOLLY. What does Dhanvantari, the mighty god of medicine, say?

OLD MAN. I'm on all sorts of remedies. Native, foreign from Sassoon Hospital. Balwantrao sent a message from Gaikwad House about some great Ayurveda doctor he knows. I've swallowed his powders and potions too. No effect. I'm planning to go to Savner. Between you and me, I don't think I'll make it back.

DOLLY. Why do you say such things, master? Your Rajasanyas is still incomplete. It does not behove you to think such thoughts. With this Spanish flu flying around, we should really be in quarantine. Sitting by the river against a high wind does no good to our health. But that is no reason to assume the worst will happen.

OLD MAN. The body is not cooperating with my writing, Shankar Kashinath. This fluctuating fever has grown addicted to my body. With every day that dawns, innumerable new stories sprout and grow in my brain. The characters talk to me ceaselessly, the good and the evil, the depraved, the heroic and the monstrous. Their politics, their family life, its joys and sorrows all course through my brain like hot streams, merge with this fever and fade when it fades, leaving behind a permanent weakness. My weakness has become like a hard scab, an armour that I can't get through. The regular pulsating of my lungs is losing time. Every sign says I am not destined to complete Rajasanyas. My shadow is growing longer before my day is done. I am ebbing away. Despite my greatest efforts, conjugal bliss too was not written in my fate, Shankar Kashinath. It passed me by.

Silence.

DOLLY. Master. Master . . .

OLD MAN (*wakes up from his reverie*). What? Shall we go?

DOLLY. Come.

They start walking away. The old man stops. He pulls out an envelope from his pocket.

OLD MAN. Here take this. (*Walks away. Dolly is left holding the envelope.*)

DOLLY (*to the audience*). That was the last time Diwakar and Gadkari, known to everybody as master, met. Gadkari died at Savner on 23 January 1919.

(*The envelope comes up on the screen. Gadkari's statue, vandalized in 2017 appears. Its shards fly about. The envelope is superimposed on them.*)

(*Dolly looks at the screen*). The inscription on the envelope read: 'Shri Shankar Kashinath Garge esquire, alias Diwakar. Please do not open this envelope during my lifetime. Seeking your good wishes. Yours, Ganesh Gadkari, Pune.' What could the envelope have contained?

Lights brighten. The old man enters.

DOLLY. Is something the matter, master?

OLD MAN. Why do you ask?

DOLLY. You've worn a scarf. (*Pause*)

OLD MAN. I went to the river. It's always windy there. There's nothing wrong with me.

DOLLY. Let's take a look. (*Feels his forehead. Gives him a glass of water from a thermos.*) Have some warm water, master. What did the envelope contain?

OLD MAN. The day after Gadkari died, Diwakar went alone to the river bank and eagerly opened the envelope. Inside, he found a slip of paper with a single line: 'A thing that has been a part of me and known me from outside in.' That thing was a bit of old silk thread. Diwakar recognized it instantly for what it was. Without a doubt, it belonged to the waist cord every male child is made to wear from birth. Diwakar's hand touched his waist and he realized he wasn't wearing his. Yet the memory of its touch and the innumerable childhood events that came with it, remained. The grief of losing his friend made him introspective, and he wrote a farewell tribute to him there and then using the master's style.

Light on Dolly. The old man is in darkness.

DOLLY. On the fifth-day puja, after a baby is born, it feels the first touch of a black cord made of fine threads spun by silkworms feeding on mulberry leaves. The cord might go around the baby's wrist or neck or ankle, but it comes finally to its resting place around the waist. Little black dots appear on the baby's cheek and forehead and palm. The tiny being, nestled against its tired mother, has no idea that the origin of the cord that hugs his waist lies in the China of thousands of years before Christ, where people noticed that silkworms feeding on mulberry leaves spun silk yarn. How is the infant to know that the entire purpose of the indestructible cocoon of tradition that binds his waist is to guard him against the evil eye? The warm protection of that silk cord stays with him as he grows older. By the time his head is ritually shaved, its presence is etched permanently in his little brain. It is now an indivisible part of his life. When his mother has finished bathing him, she sprinkles water around his head three times saying, 'No hair left on your head and your waist is bound with a silk thread.'

Pause. Dolly is in darkness. The screen lights up.

A voice like Ameen Sayani's announces, 'We are about to present a famous song from a 1946 film, Dr Kotnis ki Amar Kahani, *sung by, yes, you guessed it, Jayashribai. She not only sang the song but also played the role of a Chinese girl, Ching Lan. The hero was played by, yes oh yes, no less than Annasaheb, the director V. Shantaram. The words of the song are "Nai dulhan nai Dulhan, mein hun nanhi nai dulhan." Presenting Jayashribai in the role of the fabulous Ching Lan.'[3]*

Scenes from the film are projected, fading into the song 'Mera naam Chin Chin Choo' from Howrah Bridge.[4]

The song fades. Lights as before.

DOLLY. So? What happened then?

OLD MAN: Diwakar folded the monologue that he had written spontaneously and placed it in the envelope, along with the silk thread from Gadkari's waist cord. The envelope was to become the greatest mystery of his life.

DOLLY. I don't get it. Not a word of what you've just said has appeared in any history that I know of.

3 Available at https://ytube.io/3ZYp

4 Available at https://bit.ly/3G1yYm3

OLD MAN. My dear girl, isn't that what this lockdown play of ours is all about? So then? Take it forward.

DOLLY. Right. Here's my question. Where did you get this information and what made you choose the waist cord as your subject for research?

OLD MAN. Here's my answer: Diwakar had no idea what to do with the envelope.

DOLLY. So he kept it in his pocket and there it remained as he continued teaching at school.

OLD MAN. Diwakar was a teacher at Nutan Marathi Vidyalaya.

DOLLY. It was 1919. The Spanish flu epidemic was raging around the world.

OLD MAN. The epidemic abated in 1920.

DOLLY. The Tilak era ended the same year.

OLD MAN. If you are including Tilak, you can't leave out Gandhi.

DOLLY. I am including him. And Nehru and Ambedkar too. We don't want trouble.

OLD MAN. Correct. Let's have Tagore also.

DOLLY. Oh dear. Then we must have Balgandharva, Dinanath, Deval, Khadilkar and Phalke too! Who else?

OLD MAN. Better put in Munje, Hedgewar, Savarkar. We really don't want trouble.

DOLLY. So all these people escaped Spanish flu.

OLD MAN. Except Gokhale. He died before he could escape it. In 1915.

DOLLY. Master, how many years forward are we taking this?

OLD MAN. Till 1931, the year Diwakar died.

DOLLY. Yes, of course.

OLD MAN. Like Gadkari, Diwakar had also decided that the envelope was not to be opened in his lifetime.

DOLLY. Who did he give it to?

OLD MAN. It had to be put into trustworthy hands. It wouldn't have done for it to fall into the wrong hands.

DOLLY. So he kept the envelope safe with himself from 1919 to 1930. That year, a young teacher joined his school. He was very popular with the students and became a famous writer. His name was V. V. Bokil.

OLD MAN. When Diwakar fell ill in 1930, he called Bokil over, told him the entire history of the envelope and handed it over to him, saying . . .

DOLLY. . . . 'Bokil, please don't open it in your lifetime.' Master, we have arrived at 1931.

OLD MAN. And that's when the fun begins.

DOLLY. Forget it, master. You've spouted so much history, but why have you never said where you stand? Tell me. How come the curve of your graph suddenly flattened out after the Emergency? The Janata Party came and went. Indira Gandhi, Rajiv Gandhi, Narasimha Rao, Atal-ji—they all passed on. The Babri Masjid fell, everything began to shine after 1990. The Godhra massacre happened, riots happened, there were bombings, terrorists multiplied, malls and multiplexes proliferated. In time, 2014 arrived, followed by cows. And then bang . . . bang . . . bang and bang. There were four bangs. Four fell dead. Two in Maharashtra—in Pune and Kolhapur, and two in Karnataka. This might be history. But it is true. It is our history. Sir, your Emergency is now grandpop and great-grandpop history. Your children have left the country and gone abroad. You who appeared with the dawn of Independence are now confined to your old-people's homes, where your children show you your grandchildren and great-grandchildren on Skype.

The screen lights up. A song plays—Savarkar's 'Jayostute, jayostute, he mahanmangale shiavaspade shubhade'—accompanied by visuals.[5]

---

5 Available at https://bit.ly/3GzsvjP

The song fades.

DOLLY. Master . . .

OLD MAN (*finger on his lips*). Shhh . . . Listen

DOLLY. To what?

OLD MAN. Just listen. To the silence. Can you hear it? The silent majority? Dolly dear, there was a bang in Delhi even in the year I was born. Hey Ram. Riots. Houses burnt down. There was another bang in '84. The mother was killed in Delhi. More riots. More people dead. Then another bang in the south. The son was killed. With that, the country gave the world a humongous cracker, the human bomb, as gift. We also gave it Kashmir, Chhattisgarh, Gadchiroli, along with Khairlanji, Malegaon and the Taj Hotel. We serve up a long menu in our parts, Dolly. A multicuisine menu. We've become a veritable paradise of bangs and bombs. Everywhere in the world, the majority is always silent. The complaining voices you hear are always of the minority. It is only when the Shishupal governing the country has committed his hundred sins that the majority wakes up and does its duty at the polls. This is how it has been through history. There is no guarantee that's how it will continue to be. That's why we must be on our toes at all times. This is going to be a long lockdown. The government's pants are down and they can't get them up, try as they might. The silent majority sits in the villages, defeated, having trudged all the way home on empty stomachs. Everything is undone. An evil plan is afoot to rapidly WhatsApp the silent majority into believing that the past will soon return to rule the present. Once you have congealed the present with the potion of the past, you can relax for the next five years. During this time, keep the media spinning your yarn so the silent majority is caught in an ever-expanding web. Positions? They are all mixed up. By the time you notice that this man belongs to this side, he has been appointed to the Rajya Sabha and someone from there has managed a ticket to the Lok Sabha. Someone who has been a political worker all his life finds himself in prison as an urban naxal in his sunset years. Meanwhile people get elected by lakhs of votes using the names of those who have been responsible for bangs since 1948. With the seven colours of the spectrum from right to left keeping up a constant whirl, you end up seeing only one colour. I have lived a lifetime researching a frayed thread from a waist cord. That is my position. I am a researcher. Aren't we here to discover why I am so obsessed by this subject, Dolly? There you are. I rest my case.

DOLLY. I have nothing to say, master. You are the master of words. Word skill is a two-edged weapon. You don't need me to tell you that. The skill allows you to make meanings clear if that is what you want, or hide them if you so desire. Over the years, you have perfected the skill of declaiming quotable lines. But I haven't found in any of those (*indicates the Amazon carons*) a thermometer that will tell us if your conscience pinches you when you say them. (*Softly, to the audience*) A certain individual is enjoying the lockdown. He is going to be filled with Corona very soon. You will witness every single symptom that WhatsApp has told you about. I will fetch a shawl before his fever starts. It is about to happen before your eyes. Till then, here's something for you to while away your time.

Airline announcement: 'Ladies and gentlemen we are about to start serving refreshments. Please take your seats. Keep your chair back straight,' etc.

Immediately after, we hear the song 'Jag he bandishala'—the world is a prison—from the Marathi film Jagachya Pathivar (*On the back of the world*).[6]

---

6 Available at https://ytube.io/3ZWM

The old man enters, a scarf round his neck, a shawl over his shoulders. Dolly aims a thermal gun at his forehead to see if he's running a temperature. They sit down on two chairs.

DOLLY. This song is just right for the lockdown, isn't it? Is your throat sore? Do you have temperature?

OLD MAN. I feel a little tired. Is it cold? I guess the symptoms have begun.

The song fades. Pause.

OLD MAN. Let the game begin. Love all . . . waist cord.

DOLLY. And so Diwakar handed the envelope over to the popular young teacher, Bokil, and passed away in 1931. Bokil was at a loss to know what to do with it. He kept it in a book as a bookmark. One day, he was calling out the roll—Gokhale, Godbole, Shah, Patel, etc.—when he came to a stop at Garge. The boy stood up. Bokil asked him casually, 'Who is Shankar Kashinath Garge to you?'

OLD MAN. The boy answered, 'My father, sir.'

DOLLY. 'Aha! You are Diwakar's son. I see you've been playing hooky too often. Meet me after class. Back he went to the roll call . . . Kinkar, Purandare, Tendulkar . . . Vijay Dhondo Tendulkar? No answer. He's hooked off again. It's his Matric year. Tell him to meet me.'

OLD MAN. At the end of class, Diwakar's son met Bokil. Bokil gave him the envelope. 'Keep this,' he said.

DOLLY. The boy said, 'What is it?'

OLD MAN. 'Your father gave it to me before he left us. I doubt there is money in it. Could be a letter or some such thing. I find it too much of a responsibility.'

DOLLY. So saying, Bokil put the envelope in a copy of a book he had written and gave it to the boy.

OLD MAN. Diwakar's son didn't know what to do. Should he open the envelope or not? Should he tell the family or not? Totally confused, he left the school during his break and started walking. He came to Appa Balwant Chowk. He noticed that the matinee show at Prabhat Talkies was Charlie Chaplin's *Modern Times*. He bought a ticket and went in. There in front of him was Vijay Dhondo, playing truant. Diwakar's son couldn't concentrate on the film. He muttered, 'I'll be back in a moment' and left. When Vijay Dhondo looked for him after the show, he was gone, leaving behind Bokil-teacher's book with the envelope in it on his seat. Vijay Dhondo went to his house to return the book. Then the two boys sat by the riverside and fell into a long and serious discussion.

DOLLY. They arrived at a plan which took them to a radio-repair shop in Sadashiv Peth, next to Social Club, that is, Bharat Natya Sanshodhan Mandir. The owner of the shop was absorbed in repairing a radio. He was yet another writer. D. B. Mokashi, author of *Dev Chalale* and *Amod Sunanshi Ale*. He examined the envelope and said, 'This is a huge responsibility. Two writers, Ram Ganesh and Diwakar, are party to it. Now I suggest you go back home. Consult the family and decide what's to be done. And listen . . . if your radio ever needs repairing, I am here . . . and Charlie Chaplin's *Modern Times* is playing at Prabhat. Have you seen it?' The two boys nodded. 'So, did you get it?' The boys were silent. 'Did you realize that Chaplin is playing who he was?' Vijay Dhondo said, 'Meaning?' Mokashi said . . .

OLD MAN. 'Meaning, when an artist's own worldview seeps into the role he is playing, the work holds together as a work of art. In the language of radios, when the crackle disappears, you know you've hit the right station. Now run along you rascals . . . playing hooky to watch films.'

DOLLY. When the boys parted, Vijay Dhondo took the book home to read, with the envelope still in it. One day, he grew restless with curiosity. He couldn't sleep wondering what the envelope which he was using as a book mark, contained. So he steamed it open. He read Ram

Ganesh's single line about his waist cord. He felt the old silk thread. He realized it came from Ram Ganesh's waist cord. Instinctively, his hand went to his waist. He wasn't wearing one. He stuck down the envelope flap and switched off the light. Several days elapsed. Yet he couldn't stop thinking of Gadkari's waist cord and its touch. One day, he set off down Tilak Road, to go to Diwakar's place to return the book. Lost in his own world, he found himself walking towards Tulsi Baug. He bought two waist cords from the first shop that was selling them. When he arrived at Diwakar's house, he returned the book to his son along with one of the two waist cords. 'Wear it after your bath tomorrow,' Vijay Dhondo said. 'I plan to wear mine too.' Then he wandered off, still lost in his world. What happened then?

OLD MAN. Then Bokil-teacher retired. He gave away his books to various people. I was never much for school. I could not find a job. Around 1965, I began to help out in my father's second-hand bookshop at Appa Balwant Chowk. One day, I found that book of Bokil's in a dusty corner, the envelope in it intact. The rest, dear Dolly, is history.

The screen lights up. Projected on it is the song 'Chun chun karti aayee chidiya' from Ab Dilli Door Nahin (*1957*).[7] *The old man's face lights up. He keeps the beat. When the line 'Then came the monkey too' is sung, he acts like a monkey. Dolly plays along.*

The song fades. Lights come up again.

DOLLY. Dancing, master? Be careful. Don't advance your last day. So, that is how you found the subject for your research.

OLD MAN. Yes.

DOLLY. Weren't you interested in studies or were you simply not good at them?

---

7 Available at https://ytube.io/3ZWL

OLD MAN. What answer can I make to that at this age?

DOLLY. Right. Let's forget that. But you couldn't find a job. The bookshop didn't do well.

OLD MAN. And I didn't marry. No progeny, legitimate or otherwise. No continuity of lineage. The line ends with me and . . .

DOLLY. Leaving behind nothing but your waist cord in an envelope. Which we will get to see when you are gone . . . that is, at the end of this play. Right?

OLD MAN. I guess so. Let's see . . . my father died early. Mother lived till I was 60. She is no longer with us. But some of the jewellery she was given by her family still is. I think that's enough material for us to push the story forward.

DOLLY. Maybe. But, master, let's make your character a little more interesting for this piece of lockdown entertainment.

OLD MAN. OK, if you say so. My mother saw how crazy I was about watching film shoots. She said: you're not getting anywhere. Instead of watching film shoots all the time, at least do something in art.

DOLLY. That is why you started working as a junior artist in films.

OLD MAN. That's right. I worked in several films between 1966 and 70. I even had scenes to myself. For instance, the hero would be crossing a road and I would be the man crossing behind him. Or the heroine is in hospital. The hero rushes in. I'm sitting in the waiting room. Or the hero works in a post office. I'm among the postmen at the back, sorting out mail. There were some scenes for which both Rajabhaus would call for me. Both meaning Rajabhau Paranjape and Rajabhau Thakur. Thakur's film *Ekati* was released in 68. I was not in it. I had no role, not even in the crowd. Even then Mr Thakur gave me two passes for the premier. I took Mother to Prabhat Talkies. The song picturized on Sulochanabai started, 'Limbalon utaru kashi' . . . The audience grew still. Madgulkar's lyrics, Sudhir Phadke's composition, Suman Kalyanpur's voice, Sulochanabai's chaste face and that sewing machine . . .[8]

The screen lights up. The song comes on. Dolly goes into the wings and comes back trundling a sewing machine very much like Sulochana-bai's. She pulls out some fabric from an Amazon carton and begins to sew. The whirring of the machine blends with the song.

OLD MAN. I began to love 'mother' songs from that day on.

DOLLY. Please go on, master. What happened next?

OLD MAN. What indeed? The intermission. And then that thing happened.

DOLLY (*still sewing*). What thing, sir? People would like to know. Do tell us.

OLD MAN. In those days, vendors would enter the auditorium during the intermission and walk around selling things like dry bhel mix, peanuts, lemon drops and the like. I was about to ask Mother if I could get her something when I heard a voice calling, 'Educate your beloved child, make him clever, buy him a waist cord.' When he came to our row and spotted me, he said, 'Sir, I have survived because of you.' For a few moments I was nonplussed. But then it dawned on me that this was the man who would come begging to our shop regularly on two sacred days. Back then, along with books, I used to sell some stationery items—ink, pencils, erasers. I also kept a stock of waist cords. One day when this man came, I decided not to give him money. I gave him a bunch of waist cords instead and said, 'Why beg? Go, sell these.'

He took them and there he was, months later, at the premier of *Ekati*. Mother was curious, so I told her the story. She was astonished. She had no idea I had been selling waist cords. 'That's a good thing you're selling,' she said. Then she told me to take the Deccan Queen to Mumbai and get silk thread from Crawford Market. She would twist the thread into waist cords and charm bands for the neck and wrists. She showed me the path, and that was that. Soon, we were selling our own atmanirbhar brand of waist cords. We called them Ekata waist cord. If you talk to women who became mothers between 1968 and 90, and ask them which were the best waist cords available then in Tulsi Baug, they will say in practically one voice: if you wanted a waist cord, Ekata Brand was the one to go for. It was like ground supari. The one to go for was Joshi's Roasted Ground Supari with extra liquorice. Sadly, dear Dolly, the wheel of fate turned after 1990. The economy was liberalized. Madgulkar's rousing song declaring war against the enemies of humanity had faded. We were back to the Silk Route of pre-Christ days. Our atmanirbhar Ekata Brand waist cord fell by the wayside. In its place came Chinese waist cords and a variety of charm bands. What's that you're sewing, Dolly?

DOLLY. A mask for you, master. You'll require one a day. That's 14. (*Gravely*) If something happens to you before then, I can always donate the remaining ones to the Corona Warriors Association. They'll mask unknown noses.

Pause. Dolly rises, takes the old man's temperature with her thermal gun and makes a note of it.

OLD MAN. Once, Mother made pickles every year. Now it's masks. Dolly . . .

DOLLY. Yes?

OLD MAN. Do you finding this entertaining?

DOLLY. You need to get back on track. The premier of *Ekati* was a turning point in your life. Your mother showed you the path. Till 1990, waist-cord business. After that, the whole world became one, but you, master, withdrew more and more into yourself.

OLD MAN. I would keep thinking of that monologue Diwakar wrote as a tribute to Gadkari. That ancient silk thread woven by worms feeding on Chinese mulberry leaves would come into my dreams transformed into a Chinese dragon. I began to believe that the waist cord along with its touch and the human brain somehow formed the secret principle of life. That idea gave direction to my research and enabled me to resolve some fundamental theoretical principles. Dolly, can we have the slide show please?

The screen lights up. Dolly begins her presentation. Slides, graphics, clips illustrate her talk.

DOLLY. This research became a lifelong mission. The subject being delicate, he had to do it single-handed. Now that he has begun to show symptoms of Covid-19, he has decided to share his research with you before his end comes. My boss is not highly educated. I cannot even say that he has come up from humble beginnings, because he is actually going down both mentally and physically. He has fever. His throat is scratchy. His nose has started running. He will soon find it hard to breathe. You are familiar with the signs. So let me cut a long story short and start. In case he needs me during the proceedings, I will have to take a break to attend to him. We have arranged for songs and slogans to be projected to keep you entertained. You might find some of the things we show you nonsensical. But, given the lockdown situation, you might find them entertaining. Let us first look at a few fundamental theories that the boss has formulated:

Either the old man speaks or his recorded voice is heard saying the following lines which are projected simultaneously on the screen.

OLD MAN / VOICEOVER.

(1) Is it possible that the touch of the cord put round a child's waist during the fifth-day puja affects his ways of thinking?

(2) If that be the case, do these ways get transferred to the cells that the cord touches, whether it is at the waist, neck or wrist, at the same pace at which the brain matures?

(3) Does the touch of the waist cord remain as an illusion even after a person has stopped wearing it?

(4) If such an illusionary touch continues to be sensed on the skin that has been so touched previously, do the ways of thinking that evolve in a fully mature brain get transferred in turn to the cells proximate to those areas of skin?

(5) Would it be possible with AI—or artificial intelligence—technology to recreate in the lab a virtual waist cord using its effect on the concerned areas of the skin?

(6) If it can so be created, could a man's ways of thinking—his ideology whether leftist, rural/urban naxal, rightist or extreme rightist and whether or not he believes in religion, God, country—can be recorded with enough chromosomal facts to make it foolproof as admissible evidence in a court of law?

(7) If such a thing can be achieved, the world will become fully transparent by the end of this research. An official test conducted on a swab taken from affected skin will win over every constitution of the world's nations.

–Since this test is going to be equally applicable to all people of whatever caste, creed, community, colour, ideology, it will bring into being something that has not been dreamt of—global understanding. It will make our most private ideas public. Nothing will remain private. Nothing will be judged moral or immoral.

–The test will reveal an individual's stand on any issue without his having to declare it.

–The test will render null all fundamental rights to privacy, and determine whether an individual has remained primitive by instinct or evolved and to what extent, or has refused to evolve and continues to experience the sensation of possessing a tail.

–A law will have to be enacted to determine whether to make the test mandatory for everybody or only for those who manifest certain symptoms or to people over a certain age.

–A separate law will have to be passed after a full discussion among all parties to decide whether findings of such tests are to be kept secret or made public or linked to Aadhar cards.

–However, the fundamental issue at the moment is how nations will respond to sanctioning the research required for such a test to be created. There are bound to be differing opinions on the issue but it demands a calm discussion.

DOLLY. This is terribly theoretical and boring. Whether it will lead to anything at all is a moot question. However, there is a companion project that will afford entertainment and income. Research means funds. To raise them, it is proposed to set up an extensive amusement park on the lines of Disneyland. Research for the test will be carried on as branches of this amusement park or at science and technology parks set up in different places. We will now show you some sample visuals from one amusement park.

(*She indicates the locations of the visuals of the waist cords, arm bands and wrist bands with the aid of a pointer.*)

For instance, this section is titled:

'The History of the Waist Cord: Ancient Period'.

Silk-making process—a mulberry bush in China. Silkworm. Cocoon. Silk thread. Silk Route.

Pre-Vedic Age. A sample visual

The Greek civilization. A sample visual

The Egyptian civilization and the waist cord.

Pre-Christian Age. We see Alexander the Great. We see his statue.
We notice that he is not wearing a waist cord.
But press the button and a waist cord appears.

When you enlarge the image, you see the skin behind the waist cord.
When you enlarge that, his DNA becomes visible. Then you see charts
of his DNA and characteristics of his nature. Naturally, it is all in Greek.
But you can hear the translation through your headphones.

Here's Cyrus the Great wearing a wrist band.

This is Confucius. His neck band is hidden under his beard.

The Indus civilization. Mohenjo Daro. The famous statuette of the dancing girl, arm on hip. Her waist cord.

A painting from the Ajanta Caves. Two friends discuss the waist cord.

Sadhus selling waist cords in the Himalayas.

Sadhus with knowledge of the importance of waist cords
bathing in the Ganga.

Adivasi civilization and songs about the waist cord. (*Vaguely tribal-sounding songs in any language accompanied by random visuals.*) This song comes from the Adivasis living in Thane, India. This one comes from Andhra Pradesh and this one from Chhattisgarh.

This section is devoted to 'The Mughal Empire and the Waist Cord'. Babur reading the chapter on the waist cord in the *Baburnama*.

Humayun in his court, displaying the waist cord
that has been presented to him.

Akbar discusses the Hindu waist cord in court.

An abhang written by unknown saint poet Venugopal who belonged to
Bundelkhand and was a contemporary of Godse Bhatji who wrote the
famous eye-witness account of the 1857 uprising. The original is of
course in Bundelkhandi. But here is a free translation:

The silkworm weaves its cocoon of silk
Around my neck is its soft touch string
A whisper rises on devotees' lips
Run Vitthala run, save us, they sing
Says Venu, in the cocoon of my mind
Forever doth a silkworm reside

Now follows a section in which some Gosavi saints
flaunt their waist cords without any shame.

The next section belongs to mighty men, now deceased,
with their waist cords and arm and wrist bands:

Raja Ram Mohan Roy argues his case.

Mahatma Gandhi spins khadi yarn for waist cords.
Beside him is Vinoba Bhave.

Hitler displays his arm band in a meeting.

Winston Churchill argues that a waist cord is a foolish thing.

Tagore and Einstein state their respective sides
regarding the journey from worm to cocoon.

Nehru tells Lady Mountbatten a joke about waist cords.

Indira-ji and Pupul Jaykar discuss details regarding waist cords and wrist bands among the Warli and Santhal tribes. You will observe that Indira-ji's hand is placed on the band around her neck.

Atal-ji, Narasimha Rao and Chandrashekhar share a joke about waist cords.

Rajiv-ji listens benevolently to a discussion about waist cords and faith.

Pramod Mahajan ties a band on Atal-ji's arm.

Sushma Swaraj, Arun Jaitley and Gopinath Munde argue about wrist bands during a round-table conference.

(*The train of visuals moves forward in this fashion to present times, accompanied by suitable music. During the presentation, you hear the old man coughing. Now we come to the final visual.*)

This is how the Black Lives Matter movement began. This incident took place on 25 May 2020. The picture shows white police officer Derek Chauvin kneeling on the neck of African American George Floyd till he suffocates. His right hand is at his waist and his left in his pocket. The jury is still out on whether the officer was wearing a waist cord or not.

There are several more sections following this, but some of them are for adults only. They deal with the waist cord in man–woman relationships, Vatsyayan's commentary on the subject, the waist cord and the evolution of undergarments. But I'm going to wind up here. You must have heard my boss cough during my presentation.

(*The doorbell rings. Dolly hurries to the sewing machine, picks up a mask and covers the old man's nose and mouth. He does not protest. He tries to say something but can't be heard through the mask. She bends her ear to him.*)

Henceforth you will not be able to hear what Master is saying. We will follow the device you saw in the play *Himalayachi Savli*. I will listen to him and relay what he is saying to you. (*Softly*) Master, we need to send your Covid-test sample to the lab. (*Exit*)

Light on the old man. A song 'Aai tujhi athavan yete' (Mother, I miss you) from the play Duritanche timir javo, *begins to play.*[9] *The old man's*

---

9 Available at https://ytube.io/3awP

masked face lights up. He rises and acts out the words as Bhalchandra Pendharkar used to in the play.

Dolly enters, clad in PPE. She takes a swab from the old man's nose and leaves. The song stops and an airline announcement begins: 'Ladies and gentlemen, our plane is about to land. Please return to your seats,' etc. Dolly returns, still clad in PPE.

DOLLY. You said, didn't you, that you began to love mother-songs after the premier of *Ekati*? That's why I played this song. It is perfect for the occasion. There is also the fact that we do begin to think about our mothers in our last moments. (*Pause.*) The test report will come by email. And then?

(*The old man gestures 'and then?' Dolly bends forward to catch what he's saying.*)

I meant, what do we do when it comes? Hospital? No? You want to be at home. Ventilator? Don't want it? How will you breathe? What? Reserve it for a young patient? Right . . .

(*The old man begins to sob.*)

What's the matter, master? Please tell me. This is your last chance to speak. How can I tell you not to be afraid? Everybody fears death.

(*The old man begins to speak as he sobs. Dolly tells the audience what he is saying. His close-up as he speaks is projected on the screen. Dolly is becoming emotional but she controls herself as she interprets him.*)

What's that? Master says nothing worked. Couldn't decide where he stood. Couldn't decide which side to be on. Both sides seemed right. The shop didn't do well. Your father couldn't manage it, you couldn't manage it. Everything slipped through your fingers. Confidence. When will you get that? People would constantly ask: What? What do you want to be when you grow up. (*Pause.*) Nothing so far. Yes, it is. You're still breathing. Test result? Yes, it has come. Came a while ago. Yes, it's Covid Positive.

(*To the audience*)

I told him immediately. He has no family. Why hide it from him? Master simply couldn't make it in life. After 2014, it was downhill all the way. In the old days, for 60–70 years, we used to have a proper cocktail: left, right, socialist, revolutionary, Dalit, Maratha, Brahman— a rainbow. There was give and take. In the new system there are only two colours, black and white. Friend or enemy. Master didn't know what to do. And I didn't know what to do with him. I was new. Sir would remain silent for hours. If I asked him what he was thinking, he'd say: I'm doing research. What research, I'd ask. He'd clam up. He'd continue to think. Once in a while he would go out. If I asked him where, he would say: down to the jail. But he'd turn back at the corner, saying: I'll go day after tomorrow, not today. I asked him once why the jail of all places. He said . . . (*The old man replies and Dolly communicates it to the audience*) . . . My father's there. Please, he was there in 42. He is no longer with us. He says then: why am I still here? Who will I show my research to? With that he would burst into sobs.

(*To the old man*)

Isn't that so?

(*To the audience*)

See? He's clammed up. But he said these strange things. Actually, he's been talking a lot today because you are here. Other times with me it's just practical things. (*Pause*) See, he's growing a little breathless. He'll require oxygen soon. But he has refused to be put on a ventilator. He wants a younger patient to have it. Which means he'll soon be gone. I'll shroud him in PPE and call the Covid Warriors. They'll manage the rest. (*She gets emotional*)

I'm not a trained nurse, you know. I hope I can manage things at the end. I'm on my own here. I am rather amused at myself. As a woman, you are used to pregnancies and births. But in this play, I've had the opportunity to observe a Covid-19 death at close quarters. With you as witnesses. Actually, I've made preparations for a 14-day span as in 14 masks, etc. But it appears he's going sooner. He's gasping for breath. Master, who am I to you? Why am I here? Did you order me on Amazon? Tell me. It's not like us to get so involved with people. Sometimes I wish we had met when you were young . . . in 76. You'd have got powerful roles in films alongside me. I might even have played lead roles in your films. Or we could have taken a patent on your mother's waist cords and set up a manufacturing plant in Wuhan. You needed a companion, master. Why did you tie a band round an entire lifetime's loneliness? The envelope holding that secret will remain closed once you've gone. Come, then. Let's go in and wind up this play about your existence. I'll need your help. Will you give it?

(*The old man nods in affirmation. Dolly exits and returns with a wheelchair. She sets the old man in it and speaks as she wheels him around the stage.*)

Come, sir. It is time for the five great life forces to shut down one by one. Please signal to me when the fifth is about to shut down. But not with an open palm, please. People might take that as a sign that you stood with the Congress party. Are you ready? Let's prepare you for your death.

(*She wheels the old man to one side and dresses him in a PPE. The lights dim and a PowerPoint presentation of the five life forces appears on the screen, accompanied by a commentary in a deep and solemn male voice. The chanting of Om provides the background score.*)

DOLLY. Master, here is a brief description of the five life forces.

(*On the screen:*

Pran. This force resides in the heart and breathes.

Apaan: This force resides in the colon and is responsible for excretion.

Vyaan: This force occupies the whole body.

Udaan: This force resides in the throat and separates food from drink.

Samaan: This force resides in the navel and provides nutrition to the pulse.

The scriptures list five sub-forces too. The fifth sub-force is called Dhananjay. This force remains in the body even after death and ensures that it does not enter into the sinful corpses that inhabit the atmosphere. This force is destroyed only when the body is cremated. That is why it is our practice to cremate a body as early as possible. Om shantih shantih shantih.

(*The words on the screen fade. Dolly dresses the old man in a PPE and seats him in the wheelchair. She wheels him to the centre of the stage. The music fades.*)

This is how my master breathed his last. This is his life story. Gadkari's envelope will go with him.

(*The sound of an ambulance siren as it approaches. It stops. Dolly wheels the old man away. The siren starts again and fades away in the distance. Dolly stands alone on the stage. Silence. She removes her PPE as actors remove their make-up, standing near a table. She addresses the audience before she exits.*)

OK. I'm off. Perhaps you have been wondering about me. Who am I? Where have I come from? How can I be so aloof? What is my character all about? How am I involved with Master? Who is he? A life was born, lived and was taken away by this epidemic. What difference does it make? But it does. Every life counts, but is no longer valued. I have been able to collect a lot of data since 2014. Single lives in the future might find this data useful. I can give you a hint. In these Netflix times, take it that I am an undercover agent. A spy. (*Wickedly*)

Mind you, there are some who even call me Alexa. (*Pauses as she leaves*) Oh yes. We have set up a stall outside for the sale of Ethnic Ekata–brand waist cords, arm bands and wrist bands. We have cotton ones for people who are allergic to silk. Profits from the sale will go to the Covid Warriors. For online purchases, you may log onto waist-cordlinks.master.com. (*Pause*) See you then. I shall report for duty at the next house. (*Exit*)

The stage is empty. As the light fades, notes of Raga Bhairavi are heard on the harmonium. Blackout.

with SHANTA GOKHALE

Over the last few years, Satish Alekar has been acting in an eclectic range of films in Marathi and Hindi, from promotional films on social issues, to short fiction films, to full-length features. Cinema would appear to have become his third innings after his decades of work at Pune's Theatre Academy followed by his directorship of Pune University's Department of Performing Arts. This interview took place on 22 February 2022, when he was shooting for a film in Mumbai.

Thakishi Samvad, *which I have translated as* Conversation with Dolly, *strikes me as having a radically different trigger point from any of your earlier plays. When you have been asked about what set off the ideas for plays like* Mahanirvan, Begum Barve, Mahapur, *you have attempted to put together an answer with scraps of memory that you feel might have contributed. I have a feeling that you have a clearer answer to where* Thakishi Samvad *came from. The pandemic is only the immediate issue. There is something larger going on here. Perhaps you could talk about that?*

Yes. My world changed in 2014. For 65 years, I had walked about freely, thought freely, expressed my feelings and beliefs freely. Difference of opinion was accepted as just that—difference of opinion. Suddenly the space to do my thing, to be myself, began to shrink. To think differently became a crime. You began to be labelled anti-national, urban naxal. Dissent was no longer respected. The space for dissent was being squeezed out of existence. The trigger for this play came when four people were murdered in broad daylight and the country as a whole had nothing to say about it. Narendra Dabholkar went first. Then Govind Pansare. Then Prof. Kalburgi. Then Gauri Lankesh. What harm had they done anybody?

They were living their life quietly, and suddenly somebody decided they had no right to live? Who were these people who were allowed to take these four lives? I felt trapped. I was angry. Very angry. And restless. I had to find an outlet for my anger. Writing a play was the natural outlet for me.

entertaining? What in fact do we mean when we say that something is enter-taining? This was leading up to a definition of the function of art.

But that is not where I wanted to go. That was only an entry point. Part of my anger in these times has been with the public elevation of mindless ideas about science and history, mindless ideas that have become prevalent. Such ideas once occupied the margins—they are now mainstream. Historical facts are being subverted and replaced by fantasy. I imagine children now telling their grandfathers: that is not how it was. We have been taught at school that we invented television and we practised plastic surgery in ancient times. I wondered how I could give this kind of thing a theatrical expression. That is where the story of the mysterious waist cord, passed on from generation to generation, emerged. I have misused iconic sculptures, paintings, portraits from established museums to help my mediocre narrator bolster his arguments. That's what the new history is all about—twisting some facts and suppressing others to fit the newly constructed narrative.

But that satirized falsification of history traces a real history too. The figures in your false history are the real figures of Maharashtra's literary history. That, and the songs you have chosen, are deeply rooted in Marathi culture and consciousness.

Being culture-specific is a strength. I value it.

Coming back to the trigger: you converted your anger, frustration and lone-liness into this play. Given its political engagement and strong musical and visual content, it is supremely performable play in a very unusual form. Are you planning to stage it?

That's going to be difficult. I do not have a group of actors with me as I once did. Several members of the old group have passed on. Those who are still with us are that much older. I am older. I am not sure I have the energy to get a cast together, run rehearsals, organize shows and itineraries. The alternative is to look for a younger person who can do all this. Where do I find such a person? At the same time, you can't keep a play you have written to yourself. It cries for an audience. As a playwright too, I need a performance or at least a reading to tell me whether the play is working or not. And if not, why not. In the old days, I would have read it out to the group—the Theatre Academy actors—the very next day after it was completed. I needed to read this one out to somebody. So, I read it out to the students at the Lalit Kala Kendra where I still hold an honorary position. The reading told me the play worked. The students didn't appear to mind it. After that, I began reading it out to groups of people, generally 10 to 15.

In their homes?

In somebody's home. People invited me to do a reading and invited a few friends over to hear me. That was my audience.

What do you require for a reading?

I need a large-screen television set. Most people have that. I connect my iPad to it for the last series of visuals. I do not show the songs as visuals. I play them on my mobile. These readings have worked.

How has the feedback been?

Good. People enjoy it. They get the point. But I do have ideas for a full-fledged stage performance. I would like the images of iconic figures to leap out at the audience in the form of holograms. And the final series of visuals should appear around and above the audience. The entire theatre should be transformed into a museum. We have the technology for it. The effect would be stunning. And it would underline the idea of something real and solid being turned into an unreal fantasy.

That sounds like a plan. But until it can be realized, you will continue to do readings, won't you? That too is a form of performance.

It is. Besides, the play is also being published. For the first time in my theatre career, a play of mine is being published before it has been staged.

A BRIEF NOTE INSPIRED BY THAKISHI SAMVAD

VAIBHAV ABNAVE

There are many 'global' signposts one could name to establish the apparent contemporaneity of Satish Alekar's play, *Thakishi Samvad*—the Covid-19 pandemic, lockdown, green-red-orange zones, N95 masks, oximeters, PPE kits, Amazon parcels, WhatsApp forwards, Netflix, amusement theme parks, post-truth, AI, big data, surveillance, Alexa and imminent, lonesome, all-pervasive yet banal death. One would also be tempted to 'nationalize' the deceptive contemporaneity of this play by jotting down another series of concrete nodes—India since 2014, Modi–Shah, political polarization, state repression, endemic fear, murders of rationalists, urban Naxals, silent majority, migrant walks and democracy's march towards dictatorship. These run through the play while invoking a larger post-Independence backdrop painted with the political assassinations of the Gandhis (Mahatma, Indira, Rajeev), the Emergency, liberalization and persistent brutality (from Kashmir to Khairlanji). Further, one could historicize the cultural specificity of this play by putting together one more series of actual names—the Spanish flu in Pune, Shaniwar Peth, Kasba Peth, Omkareshwar, the Mula-Mutha rivers, Ram Ganesh Gadkari, Shankar Kashinath Garge aka Diwakar, Vijay Tendulkar, D. B. Mokashi and kargota (silk thread). For many, this would make it a quintessential Alekari or Alekar-esque play. One might feel thrilled to discover that the kargota, an otherwise insignificant ritual object, not only ties together all three—the global, the national and the local—but is also conferred a 'world-historical' significance through the grand history of great men, Alexander to Amit Shah. It is also granted a universal anthropological status through the ongoing research of the narrator-protagonist, 'professionally' demonstrated by using a PowerPoint presentation.

After connecting all the referential dots and space-time coordinates, one might feel gratified at having situated Alekar's play historically, culturally and politically and having found, at the same time, a key to unlock its mystery—the silk thread that connects the global, the national and the local. All three are delicately interwoven in the play along with interludes of popular Hindi-Marathi songs and inflight announcements. It might give us a sense of satisfaction to have discovered in *Thakishi Samvad* a truly contemporary play, one that is at once globally relevant, authentically Indian and deeply rooted in the specific subcultural Puneri Marathi ethos.

However, one's complacence is short lived. One soon realizes that this exhaustive survey of referential coordinates barely scratches the elusive, slippery surface of the play-text. At best, it tells us something about its subject and the multiple contexts it invokes. But it does not even begin to engage with the form-content[1] of the play-text, with what Alekar *does* with these multiple referential contexts, how he *plays* with them using artistic means singular to theatre. It only answers the question: what makes Alekar's play contemporary, thus conflating the singular contemporaneity of his play-text with mere contexuality, understood in a historicist sense. It reduces the subjective, speculative contemporaneity of Alekar's play-text to an objective, empirical contexuality.

To engage with the form-content and the theatre-thinking[2] of this play-text, one needs to raise a more crucial question: what is Alekar's play-text contemporaneous to? Anyone who is familiar with his theatre[3]

1 I borrow this formulation from poet-playwright-critic Dr Rajeev Naik's Marathi formulation 'roopashaya', proposed during a lecture at Aksharnandan, Pune, in 2019.

2 I borrow this term from activist Alain Badiou. For a detailed discussion, see Rhapsody for the Theatre (Verso, 2013) and In Praise of Theatre (Polity, 2015).

3 I mean both his key play-texts—one-acts as well as two-acts—and their performances directed by Alekar himself in some of which he has played key characters.

must undoubtedly have experienced a formal and thematic resonance cutting through his singular theatrical constellation spanning more than five decades.

As an aside, I would like to add something else about this resonance. I have been in the audience for one of Alekar's performed readings of *Thakishi Samvad*, which gave me a clue to how the text would appear and sound on stage. Even before that, when I read the play-text, I had heard his distinct tone transmitted vividly through the typed words, an experience I have had before while reading his other play-texts as well. It is as if the written word already anticipates and condenses the sonic tonality on paper, like a musical score-sheet, a written performance; while the sonic utterances play out his writerly precision through actors' bodies, like performed writing. In short, Alekar's voice is at once written and sonic, a text-performance. It is obvious then that the question of contemporaneity cannot be confined only to *Thakishi Samvad*. It must be elevated to the level of Alekar's theatrical constellation itself.

What is Alekar's theatre contemporaneous to? A provisional hypothesis[4] I propose is as follows: Alekar's theatre is contemporaneous to the ongoing and seemingly endless *interregnum*[5] inaugurated by modernity. Let me briefly elaborate what I mean by this. On the one hand, modernity dislocates, abandons the seemingly settled world of tradition and opens up an abyss. On the other hand, this abyss, instead of being readily filled by 'another world', gives way to contesting, conflictual visions and a ceaseless search for what this 'other world' could (should) be. How is it to be created, who will create it and to what end? The old world of tradition continues to end endlessly while the new world of modernity is not yet in sight. Interregnum names this suspended passage *in-between*. Alekar's theatre of in-betweenness is at once non-didactic and anti-romantic, even while it uses formal tools commonly associated with didactic theatre and

4 This provisional formulation is inspired by Dr Rajeev Naik's recent article 'Alekari Natya-avakaash' (Mukta Shabd, Diwali 2021).

5 I borrow this term from the Marxist thinker-activist Antonio Gramsci's Selections from the Prison Notebooks (1971).

transmits an intensely unnameable experience usually equated with romanticism[6]. This is a disjunctive combination[7]—non-didactic yet anti-romantic. Alekar creates a singular theatrical experience of the oscillation between indecision and yearning, ending and endlessness. He concretizes it by creating a singular theatre form that oscillates between existence and in-existence, reality and dream, actual and virtual[8]. His theatre gives duration to this elusive experience of in-betweenness by sustaining a dialectical tension between each of these pairs without letting them collapse into each other.

I would like to conclude my provisional formulation by reflecting on the third pair that occurs in *Thakishi Samvaad*—the actual and the virtual. The Covid-19 pandemic which provides a crucial referential context to the play, has brutally exposed the increasing virtualization of our lives, where the virtual is not only uncoupled from the actual but also stands in as a substitute for it. This substitution has compelled theatre to surrender to the new regime of virtuality, to the new normalcy of digital theatre, which many happily celebrate as a new genre of theatre. Against this backdrop which decouples the here from the now, privileges nowness[9] over hereness, thus taking away the essential precondition for theatre to take place, *Thakishi Samvad* has to be read/heard/seen and *thought*, as a political intervention to re-ignite the desire for theatre, the desire for an actual encounter with finite-mortal bodies and, through this encounter the desire to be infected with immortal theatre-thought. In this play, Alekar playfully alerts us to the virtualization of theatre, by frequently casting doubt on whether it is *actually* taking place on stage before us or being

6 I draw upon Alain Badiou's conceptualization of 'didactic' and 'romantic' from his Handbook of Inaesthetics (Stanford University Press, 2004).

7 It is this disjunctive combination that sets Alekar's theatre-thinking apart from that of his contemporary, Mahesh Elkunchwar.

8 Following Dr Rajeev Naik's suggestion, one could also add 'high/classic/elite and low/folk/popular' (Alekari Natyavakash, Mukt Shabd, Diwali 2021, p. 73).

9 In this decoupling, nowness gets equated with liveness, where virtual simultaneity takes over actual-bodily encounter.

virtually relayed on some digital platform without necessitating our presence. Yet, he also re-configures the tension between actual and virtual, mainly through Thaki's character. Who is Thaki? She could be an android named Alexa, who is immune to mortality, immune to dreams-memories-guilt-indecisiveness-fear-anxiety-yearning; in short, immune to everything which makes the abyssal experience of in-betweenness possible. Instead, she is endowed with techno-immortality, with digital memory as data. In short, she is gifted with a kind of techno-transcendence. Yet, by the very virtue of being-*in*-theatre, her existence is split between being-a-character (virtual) and being-an-actor (actual). Via the finite-mortal body of an actor who-would-play Thaki, she will be exposed to the inescapable experience of in-betweenness, the experience of indecisiveness-yearning-ending. Like Thaki, we too, who are comfortably enjoying the techno-transcendence of digital theatre, will be exposed once more to this inescapable in-betweenness. The question is, will this actual bodily encounter *in* theatre cure Thaki (and us) of techno-transcendence? Will this encounter infect her (and us) with the desire for theatre? Will this encounter tear apart Thaki's body (and our bodies) opening it to immortal theatre-thought? And, in some not-so-distant future, like Thaki, if we were to attain techno-immortality, as many of us already desire, then in the absence of finite-mortal bodies, will there be theatre? In other words, would immortal theatre-thought exist without finite-mortal bodies? When faced with these questions, Alekar's play quietly suggests, 'let us wait a bit more, we are still in-between to know answers to these questions with any certainty. Till then, let's keep playing this game of theatre. Let us sustain the duration of this in-betweenness'. That is how Alekar transmits the desire for theatre even through his performed reading of the play.

Pune, 1 April 2022

VAIBHAV ABNAVE is an independent researcher and filmmaker. He has taught courses in international politics, documentary film making and theatre studies at various educational institutes in India. His films—*Blur* (2008) and *Monologue* (2013)—have been shown at various international film festivals. He is presently finishing a new docu-fiction feature titled *I Am Only Making a Report.*